ONTENTS

	page		page
Preamble	1	Religious Figures	20
Nottinghamshire Churches		List of included described churches	21
- *their range*	2		
- *their furnishings*	7	Architectural Periods and Styles	66
- *wall paintings*	12		
- *monuments*	13	Glossary	66
Nottingham Alabasters	16	Bibliography	70
Churchyards	18		
Nonconformist Chapels and Meeting Houses	19		

NOTE: Throughout the text a capital C and a number denotes centuries, thus - C10 indicates Tenth Century.

PREAMBLE

The English parish church makes a significant contribution to the appearance of the countryside and the town scene. Most are of ancient fabric and are an important thread in the history of England. Unlike any other buildings, so many parish churches have been on the same site and in continual use for nearly a thousand years - some longer. In all that time they have encompassed the hopes and fears of people, inspired love and veneration, but have also been abused by the iconoclasts of the Reformation, and in the following century by the Puritans. They are established on ancient holy ground and were built for prayer and tribute. While churches were frequently built as statements of power and prestige by lords in the countryside and merchants and guilds in towns, they were at the same time expressions of piety and faith in the glory of their God. The peasant had little to give, only dues to his lord, and hard labour as an expression of his faith.

The church had a pivotal role in mediaeval life, very difficult for us to appreciate in today's world. Although, arguably, parish churches are no longer the primary or sole centres of the social and religious hearts of their communities, they are nevertheless still of appreciable importance in these respects. Churches have seen generations of creative and dedicated workmanship. At their finest they represent some of man's greatest aspirations and achievements. They are buildings of purpose, but at the same time are works of art.

At the time of the Reformation there were some 46,000 churches across the country, in addition to Cathedrals and Monastic ones. Each village and even small hamlets had a church. About half this number survive today. They were built over only a few centuries by a small population estimated at around 2 million in 1086 (the time of the Domesday Book) rising possibly to about 7 million by 1349 when the Black Death caused a reduction in the population. But out of this difficult time of the mid C14 developed one of the most wonderful and beautiful architectural forms, exclusively English and known as the Perpendicular style due to its vertical emphasis. It was the peak of mediaeval endeavour. With great boldness and astonishing skill lofty arcades were built new, or inserted in old walls. Vast windows with huge areas of glass supported by delicate tracery pierced the stonework. Splendid examples are St Mary's, Nottingham and St Mary Magdalene's, Newark. This wonderful development was brought to a halt by the Reformation and there was a long pause in years before there was much more church building, and then largely of a quite different character, in classical style in the later C17 and C18.

The creation and building of mediaeval churches was a great act of faith and effort by poor and largely illiterate people. Their life was hard, rough and laborious, they were concerned just to survive. The simplest church was luxurious compared with their rude dwellings. The greater churches must have appeared awesome. Itinerant masons and carpenters executed the more complex work on smaller churches, large churches needed a resident lodge of masons. Basic work in raising the walls was done by local men in whatever time could be spared from work in the fields.

Building knowledge was rudimentary and largely trial and error. Considerable physical effort was involved in dragging stone to site over rough tracks, and in hauling and lifting huge timbers for roofs.

When we visit a mediaeval church it takes enormous imagination to try to see it as it was in the Middle Ages.

Early mediaeval churches were generally lime washed all over outside - sometimes over plastered walls. Window and door openings were picked out in colour, reddish-brown or yellow. The brightness of the exterior contrasted with the interior, which on entering would have seemed very dark. Early windows were small and often unglazed, letting in only limited light. As times progressed windows steadily increased in area until churches became gloriously light in the late Perpendicular period. Inside, the walls were plastered and painted with pictorial biblical scenes in deep rich colours. Sculpture such as the Easter Sepulchre at Hawton would have been picked out in colour, as would arches and columns, still to be seen in surviving fragments at Blyth. Interiors would have appeared empty, no pews, stalls, pulpit, lectern, or communion rails. The nave floor would be dried earth covered with rushes or straw, but there might be some stone paving or tiles in the chancel. The only fittings would be the font with its locked cover, a stone altar table, and an oak chest for keeping money, vestments, plate and other valuables. At the entrance to the chancel, the dividing line between the sanctuary of the priest and the people's nave, was the screen with the Great Rood, the crucifix with carved figures on either side, set on a beam. In the south wall of the chancel would be a piscina in which the priest would wash his hands and cleanse the chalice and paten used in the Sacrament. Adjacent was usually a sedilia, stone seats recessed in the wall for the priest and his assistants. In the north wall opposite would be a locked cupboard called an aumbry, for safe keeping of the communion vessels.

NOTTINGHAMSHIRE CHURCHES

- *their range*

Pre-Conquest

Like most places in England, any attempt to define the early history of Christianity in the area of Nottinghamshire is beset with difficulty. Certainly the area was nominally Christian from the accession of King Paeda of Mercia in 654, although many pagan ideas continued to be converted and absorbed into the traditions of the new faith. The invasions by marauding Danes caused disruption of the Christian faith in the C9 and C10, but it did not necessarily disappear altogether. Nevertheless it is generally accepted that the Church in the Nottinghamshire region was more or less refounded as part of the Archdiocese of York in the mid C10.

The foundation of Southwell Minster in 956 was part of this, when Eadwig, King of the English, made a grant of Southwell to Archbishop Oskytel who then created a minster church with a group of clergy to serve it.

The system of preachers going out from minsters had developed at an earlier date and proved very effective for spreading Christianity among a pagan population, and for their conversion. From the minster's, daughter churches were founded; some retaining dependency and others developing independence. Also, from about the C9 local lords began building churches to serve their own estates, thus gradually infilling a network of churches.

By 1014 four kinds of churches were recognised: the chief minsters (or cathedrals), main minsters, daughter churches with rights of burial, and field churches established by local landowners, without rights of burial. From this pattern developed the parish system, not fully established by the time of the Norman Conquest in 1066 but well on the way.

Vast Perpendicular window, Southwell Minster

Eighty-five Nottinghamshire churches are mentioned in the Domesday Book and were therefore in existence by 1086. This does not signify that all these were of pre-Conquest origin, since, for instance, Holy Trinity, Ratcliffe-on-Soar was built between 1066-86. Also there are names missing from the Book where there is clear evidence of pre-Conquest remains on the site. For example, there are remains of Saxon crosses at Hawksworth, Kneesall, the great shaft at Stapleford, plus a foliated cross slab at Bilsthorpe and the remarkable Saxon coffin lid at Hickling.

Shelford is listed in the Book and there we can see a fascinating Saxon relief carving of the Virgin with Child and on the reverse an angel holding a book. It is possible that where a cross or other fragment survives, there may only have been a simple wooden church cell at the time of the survey, hardly worthy of reckoning in the list.

Although Carlton-in-Lindrick and Clayworth

Part of Saxon cross, Hawksworth

Saxon carving of Virgin and Child, Shelford

churches appear to have standing Saxon type fabric, we cannot be certain these remains are pre-Conquest due to some overlap of Saxon building characteristics into the Norman period. Carlton-in-Lindrick is mentioned in the Domesday Book, while Clayworth is not. Neither is the former St Peter's, Flawford (near Ruddington) nor St Mary's, Plumtree mentioned, under both of which, Saxon church foundations have been excavated. But, East Bridgford is mentioned and foundations of a cruciform Saxon church have also been found there. The later Norman chancel also survives at this church.

Norman

There was much new building and rebuilding in the late C11 and C12. An increasing population needed larger buildings. Many Saxon buildings would be considered inadequate in size and facilities by the Normans. There was also the building of more "field churches" by the new local lords, developing and extending a parish system.

There is more significant Norman architecture in the county than people generally realise. Blyth Priory Church with its early Norman work, late C11 and very austere, contrasting with the grandeur of the early C12 nave of Southwell Minster and the late C12 Worksop Priory (originally called Radford Priory) with its long, busily decorated nave. There are fine arcades at South Scarle and the Collingham churches. Early C12 sculptured tympana survive at Everton, Hoveringham and Southwell - from their designs they have characteristics of Saxon work and are therefore best considered as Saxo-Norman. At Hawksworth is a very unusual tympana almost barbaric in character - with deep cut concentric rings of stars and roses, a central cross and crucified figures. It bears the Latin inscription "Walter and his wife Cecilia had this church built . . .". Several churches have substantial fabric from the Norman period in their towers - St. Mary the Virgin, Plumtree; St. Peter's, Mansfield; SS Peter and Paul, Warsop. All Saints, South Leverton has an almost wholly Norman west tower with only the top modified in the perpendicular period. A number of churches display herringbone stonework, a feature of early Norman work, with examples at Averham, Laneham, East Leake and Wysall. Sookholme, Littleborough and Carburton are delightful surviving examples of tiny aisle-less Norman churches, probably not enlarged because their populations didn't expand. There are in excess of fifty Norman doorways - the one at Teversal being especially individual, and the one at Balderton is of particular excellence. There are some 30 Norman fonts. Fine ones decorated with arcading can be seen at Screveton, Bole and Woodborough. One of the finest in the county came from the former Lenton Priory and can now be seen in Holy Trinity church, Lenton. In Tollerton church is a now rare shaft piscina.

Norman tympanum, Hawsworth

Norman font, Lenton

Built into the upper part of the tower at St Wilfrid's, Calverton, are eight important panels representing rural occupations of the months through the year - feasting in January, hoeing in June, reaping in August. They possibly all came from a now lost late Norman doorway.

Gothic

Churches of this form in the county are delightful in their range and variety. There are few especial Nottinghamshire individualities apart from those with ribbed stone porch roofs, and towers with eight or more pinnacles. Of the latter, Upton near Southwell has nine pinnacles, St Mary's, Nottingham has eight. Sturton-le-Steeple, despite its name has no steeple, but has an amazing twelve pinnacles on its tower. The more typical Nottinghamshire church tower tends to be short and solid as at All Saints, Babworth. Tall spires are few, but St Mary Magdalene, Newark has a fine one, with another nearby at St Giles, Balderton. All Hallows, Gedling has one of the most exceptional steeples in the county, both visually and architecturally, the spire rising as high again as its tower, with the slight entasis on the sides of the spire having a curious exotic effect.
The whole steeple was built complete in 1300-20.

There are at least eight churches with stone roofed porches, most of them with internal ribs, including Misson, West Retford, St. Mary's, Nottingham, Bunny, East Drayton. The latter church of St Peter and St Paul is a good example of a very complete Nottinghamshire late mediaeval exterior.

Church porches are little regarded these days, everyone's objective being the inside of the church either for use or just visiting. In mediaeval times the porch was of considerable importance for the community and in liturgical terms. Its ancestor was the narthex - when the main doorway had been at the west end, and where the people had been able to watch the first part of the mass. By the middle of the C11 the main doorway had moved round to the south side of the nave. Few porches were built before the C13, which is perhaps surprising since the main doorway was the beginning point of several important church ceremonies. The service of baptism began there as did the wedding service. Only when married did the couple go into church for the nuptial mass. Porches also served as courts for minor offences, for business transactions and village meetings, hence the stone-benches along the inside.
The English climate, and an increasing need for this covered space probably caused the introduction of the porch.

Within the porches are interesting doors - mediaeval ones at South Muskham, and with fine ornate scrolly ironwork at Attenborough, Hickling and St Catherine's, Teversal.

There is magnificent work from the Early English Period c.1240 in the choir at Southwell Minster, the Lady Chapel at Worksop Priory, and the wonderful late west front of the former priory church at Newstead. The glorious chapter house at Southwell with its exquisite undercut foliage is a little later, transitional work of c.1295.

Of the Decorated period is the outstanding pulpitum (or stone rood screen) c.1320-40 at Southwell. The incomparable chancel at Hawton c.1330 with its Easter Sepulchre, Founder's Tomb Recess, sedilia and piscina is contemporary and likely to be by the same master sculptor masons as Southwell. There are good windows and interiors to be seen at Car Colston, Epperstone and Woodborough. There is particularly flowing tracery in windows at Cromwell, Sibthorpe, North Leverton - and a wonderfully sinuous east window at Hawton.

Sinuous Decorated east window, Hawton

Easter sepulchre, Hawton

The Perpendicular period (roughly 1350-1500) gave us the splendid examples of St Mary's, Nottingham and St Mary Magdalene's, Newark, a fine tower at Hawton and a tall dominant one with eight pinnacles at Greasley. East Markham has a splendid big village church of a scale more usual in East Anglia but rare in Nottinghamshire. Perhaps the most rewarding example in the county of a late mediaeval village church, is St Giles's in out of the way Holme-by-Newark. Apart from the low tower with its squat broad spire, the rest is largely a rebuild in Perpendicular style of the early Tudor era. Holy Trinity, Lambley is almost entirely Perpendicular, all of a piece, built c.1470 from a bequest in the will of Ralph Cromwell, Lord Treasurer of England. Also worth a visit is the Early English nave and clerestory of 1490 at St Michael's, Laxton, built by Archbishop Rotherham of York. There is a quite splendid set of large gargoyles to be seen along each parapet of this nave.

Tudor and Jacobean

There is little late Tudor or Jacobean work to be found in the county's churches other than some interesting interior features and monuments.

Georgian

There are delightful Georgian churches at West Stockwith (1722) and Rempstone, which has a complete village church of 1771-73 with Gibbsian rustications to its classical windows. The Church of The Holy Rood at Ossington, by John Carr, dates from 1782. There is a treasurable "Gothick" rebuild at Papplewick of 1795, for the Hon. Frederick Montague (who built the Hall) complete with the squire's pew and its fireplace. A plain red brick church at Kinoulton of 1793 was erected at the expense of the Earl of Gainsborough. Perhaps the most curious is the combined church and Newcastle Mausoleum of 1832 at Milton, near West Markham, designed by the eminent architect Sir Robert Smirke. An urban design looking out of place in a field.

Victorian

There are quite a number of churches 'restored' during the Victorian era and not a few scraped and unsympathetically over-restored. But there are also some new ones of the period, each individual and good: St Barnabas's, the Roman Catholic cathedral in Nottingham (1842-4) by Pugin, St Mark's at Mansfield (1897) with a fine interior by Temple Moore. At Daybrook there is St Paul's (1892) designed by J L Pearson; and topping the ridge on Mansfield Road, Nottingham is St Andrew's (1869) dominant and prosperous Victorian work by William Knight. St John's (1876) Perlethorpe by Anthony Salvin is a fine big church for the Thoresby estate village, given by the 3rd Earl Manvers. Possibly the most outstanding, in a fine romantic setting, is the splendid church at Clumber (1886-9) built for the Duke of Newcastle as a private chapel for the house, (now gone), and designed by Bodley and Garner. The screen, organ case and pulpit (1897) at St. Mary's Egmanton, are distinguished works by (Sir) Ninian Comper.

furnishings

There are some thirty or so ancient screens, in infinite variety with few common features. The one in St. Giles's, West Bridgford is C14, an uncommonly early survivor. The best preserved is possibly that in All Saints', Strelley, of C15 work. The screen before the Mering Chapel in All Saint's, Sutton-on-Trent of c.1510, is especially elaborate with delicate carved tracery, and an overhanging gallery-like loft. There are other fine ones in St Giles's at Balderton, Barton-in-Fabis, Hawton, Laxton, Egmanton, St Mary Magdelene's in Newark, and Holy Trinity at Wysall.

Screen by Comper, Egmanton

There are delightfully complete C17 and C18 interiors in several churches - at Barnby in the Willows, Elston, Owthorpe, and Papplewick with its side gallery. All Saints', Rempstone is a complete village church of 1771-72 with much of its interior furnishings intact. Tythby, Teversal and Winkburn are special with their Jacobean/Georgian box pews, panelling, and two or three decker pulpits. St. Catherine's, Teversal has a splendid squire's pew, large and roomy with a canopy set over, and pegs for tricorn hats. Holy Trinity, Tythby is curious, with Victorian furnishings on the north side; the south side maintained by Cropwell Butler (which has no church), still retains its box pews and two decker pulpit.

There are mediaeval misericords with all their skillfully carved variety of figures, morality

Owl and rat misericord, Newark

and humour. These can be found in St Mary Magdalene's, Newark and in Southwell Minster. Those in St. Stephen's, Sneinton are late C15 and removed there from St Mary's, Nottingham in 1848. There is other seating in variety - from plain solid oak mediaeval pews in Hawton, to delightful carved poppy headed bench ends in St Giles's Holme, Hickling, and St Giles's, Balderton, and at Sutton-cum-Lound. In All Saints' Sutton-on-Trent the bench ends have intriguing faces of bearded men and smiling women.

Poppyhead, Holme-by-Newark

Prior to the C15 the only place to sit down in church was on stone benches along the walls, as in Southwell Minster, and sometimes around the bases of the arcade piers. Usually these were only used by the sick and elderly, everyone else stood or knelt during the services. When sermons became a regular part of church services simple bench seats came to be provided, as in All Saints', Hawton. In St Nicholas's, Hockerton are benches with ends as late dated as 1599, the

8

first seating in that church. In the later C17 "horse box" pews came into fashion, with high sides and doors. Inside there was padding on the benches and cushions. These made the long sermons of the time, in unheated churches, much more bearable. The higher your status the better the pew. The Squire or Lord of the Manor had often had the added comfort of a fireplace in his pew as at Papplewick. The poor sat at the back of the church on plain benches. Pews became numbered and sometimes pew rent was charged. A number were usually kept free for the poor. Some pews in All Saints', Babworth still bear the legend FREE. There were often disputes over private pews,. At South Leverton in 1638 it was alleged Alexander Sampson "hath made a seate in our church that is not uniforme. It is higher than any other that is near unto it, and it continues still so high that it hideth the sight of the deske and the Altar from all them that sitt behinde itt."

There are diverse altar rails in Nottinghamshire churches. Of interest are early C17 ones with twisted 'barley sugar' balusters, known also as 'Laudian' from the influence of Archbishop Laud during his earlier time as Dean of Gloucester. Sanctuary rails were first introduced just after the Reformation when rood screens with their gates were removed. They were put in to keep dogs from violating the sanctity of the sanctuary and communion table, at a time when it was still common for people to bring their dogs into church with them - "the Rayle be made near one yarde in height so thick with pillars that doggs may not gett in." It was found that these rails could be useful to provide kneeling communicants with support during the Eucharist. They eventually became modelled purely for this purpose and to define the sanctuary. There are Laudian rails in Gonalston, Flintham and Lambley.

In 1076 it was decreed that all churches must be provided with a stone altar. A supported stone slab was installed, consecrated in five places by the Bishop. To add to the importance of churches, relics of saints were obtained and would be installed beneath these altar tables. The Reformation ended this, relics were cleared out and most stone altar tables removed from the churches. Plain wooden tables were installed in place as communion tables. A Jacobean table survives in the south transept of Worksop Priory and there is one of the late 1630's in St. Catherine's, Teversal.

St. Peter's, Oxton has a prie-dieux of 1681 and in St Mary's, Car Colston, is an early C16 pillar type almsbox. St Oswald's, East Stoke, has an ancient C13 parish chest. There were several uses for chests in churches - they would contain the parish records, plate for the sacrament might be put there if there was no aumbry, and sometimes they could be used for vestments. Usually a church chest had three locks, so it could only be opened when the priest and both churchwardens were present.

The earliest surviving pulpits in England are late C14. Few pre-Reformation ones have survived because the sermon was not then part of the regular church service. Sermons were not encouraged until James 1st reign and only in 1603 was it decreed that all churches should be provided with pulpits. There is a rare early wooden one surviving in Holy Trinity, Wysall from about 1400. In St John of Jerusalem's, Winkburn, is a fine C17 three decker pulpit with nice carved panels, and an elegant moulded tester over, supported on scrolly consoles. At Teversal is a combined pulpit and reading desk of about 1638. Pulpits were sometimes fitted with wheels so that their position could be adjusted for the congregation to hear the sermon. It is reputed that at Kirklington a C19 parson occasionally had his pulpit wheeled outside for a 'hide' for duck shooting!

All Saints', Barnby-in-the-Willows has rare early C17 panelling surrounding the altar in the sanctuary.

There is a pretty brass candelabra in the chancel of Holy Trinity, Wysall. It was given for the use of the 'Psalm Singers' in 1773 so that 9 men were enabled to practice their singing. Hymns were not commonly sung until the C19, but Psalms were essential to the service.

Every church has its font, almost always just inside the main door. The door is entry into the church and Baptism is entry to Christian sacraments. There are fonts in Nottinghamshire churches in great variety and of all dates from the Norman era to the present day. Of outstanding interest is the mid-C12 one from the great Lenton Priory, now in the later Holy Trinity church of 1880. It is rectangular, its sides carved with Christ's Baptism, Crucifixion and Resurrection. All Saints', West Markham is also special, it has a tub shaped Norman font carved around with arcades and with barbaric figures in each panel. St Mary's, Lowdham, has an exceptional font of about 1300, octagonal with crocketted gables on each face all supported on a central pillar surrounded by seven small columns with carved capitals. Whatton has an ornamented font typical of the date 1662 inscribed on its column - curiously this in turn stands on the inverted bowl of an earlier font set into the floor.

Norman Font, West Markham

St Mary Magdalene's at Newark has the oddity of a C15 base, with a bowl added in 1660 as a replacement for destruction during the Civil War. Each part different in its architectural character. At St Nicholas's, Tuxford is a contemporary font of 1662. Suspended over is a magnificent carved, galleried and pinnacled oak canopy also dated 1673.

Sedilia are stone seats in the chancel for the priest and his assistants. They are commonly in a set of three formed into the south wall and may have fine stone carved decoration. The one to be seen in All Saints', Hawton, is of exceptional quality for a smaller parish church.

Occasionally, and more rarely, priests' sedilia could be free-standing. There is a group of three of these stone seats arranged in front of the Mering Chantry in the chancel of St. Mary Magdalene's, Newark.

Reredos have not survived in early form in the county. There is a splendid one c.1660 in oak at St Leonard's, Wollaton, very rare in a parish church, a classical composition in three parts - fluted Corinthian columns to the centre with a broken pediment above. The great one in St. Mary Magdelene's, Newark glows with bright gilding and painted saints in the panels in mediaeval form. It is of as recent date as 1937 and was designed by Sir Ninian Comper. The reredos in St Mary's, Clifton is earlier and dates from restoration work by G F Bodley in 1884. It is of alabaster in five panels with the central one raised - Christ is displayed on the cross in the centre with saints in relief in the other panels - all fine detailed work enhanced with blue and gold, following an older tradition.

Organs were few before the Restoration and only began to come in during the C18 in the richest churches. Snetzler was a famous C18 organ builder and an elegant organ case by him can be seen in St Peter's, Nottingham. In many churches well into the C19 parishioners formed small bands on flutes, violins, bassoons and a serpent, or whatever other instruments could be obtained as accompaniments for singing. These players were often accommodated in a gallery at the west end of the church like the one at Teversal, so that during singing the congregation turned literally to 'face the music.'

A typical church account of the 1740's includes:

"1742 For hairing the bow of the viole 8d"
"1751 Gave Ben Jones to buy Reeds for the Basoon 3s 0d."

Vamping horns were used in some churches, acting as a sort of megaphone for principal singers of the choir to project their voices to give encouragement to the congregations singing where there was no band or organ. Only about eight examples are known to survive, two of which are in the county - at St. Mary's, East Leake, and at St Helen's, South Scarle. They look formidable and we can only wonder what the music in church sounded like at that time.

Easter sepulchres are representations of the tomb of Christ. Most were made of wood and were brought out of store and set up on the north side of the chancel for Good Friday. The Host was ceremonially placed in an image of Christ and then placed in the tomb, with a candle burning before it until Easter morning, when it was taken out with more ceremony in the Service. Sometimes stone sepulchres were built into the Chancel north wall. Some are simple recesses with relief carving around. An elaborate one of six bays was built in Lincoln Cathedral in about 1300, gabled and pinnacled, with the founder's tomb incorporated. This precedent led to others of which the wonderful example at All Saints', Hawton is the finest, with its founder's tomb incorporated, and carved by craftsmen

Part of Easter Sepulchre, Sibthorpe

who created the superb choir screen at Southwell Minster. A lesser example can be seen in St Peter's, Sibthorpe, and the remains of a severely damaged one in St Mary's, Arnold. The ceremony had a strong appeal in mediaeval times; the practice was not abandoned until after 1560.

wall paintings

The principal and probably only survival in the county is at Blyth. The great Doom Painting, only recently discovered and conserved, has been described authoritatively as "the most important one known in the north of England." Wall paintings were common in mediaeval times. They were designed to enlighten and exhort the mainly illiterate populace to follow the teachings of the church. In some churches a representation of the Last Judgement or Day of Doom was painted round the chancel arch - the division between the people's part of the church and the priest's. Christ is depicted in glory sitting in judgement, flanked by angels - one with the trumpet. The apostles are often incorporated and sometimes other saints. Mankind is divided into those on the left side ascending to Heaven, and on the right, those suffering the pain of the damned, descending into Hell. The awfulness depicted intended to frighten sinners into mending their ways. The right hand side tends to offer greater imaginative scope to the painter. There are also fragmentary pieces of masonry wall painting at the end of the south aisle and high up in the nave of this church.

In St Mary Magdalene's, Newark are two C16 painted panels of the 'Dance of Death' on the Markham Chantry. This is believed to be one of only two surviving in England. The idea of death levelling all the conditions is an ancient concept. The paintings portray both a salutory warning and a vision of Christian hope.

painted, stained and coloured glass

Ancient glass survives in Nottinghamshire churches mainly in fragments, due to the destruction by C16 and C17 iconoclasts. The most satisfying visually is probably the south east chapel east window of the chancel of St Mary Magdelene's, Newark, reordered from parts of several windows in 1957 by Joan Howson - two main panels of painted glass of c.1300 and others of the early C15. There is a varied collection of C13 to C15 glass in Southwell Minster, but again it is fragmentary. There are four important lower lights there in the east window of C16 French glass brought from Paris in the early C19. In St Mary's church, Greasley are mediaeval roundels of St Agatha and St Lucy, slight and tantalising remains from the little that is left of the Carthusian Priory of Beauvale. In St Michael's, Halam, are complete C14 figures of St Christopher and St Blaise, together with Adam and Eve. At St Giles's, Holme-by-Newark, John Barton filled the east window with late C15 glass. This was carefully reassembled in the 1930's. Here included is an early C14 fragment of the Coronation of the Virgin from the abandoned old church at Annesley. But for its size, St. Gregory's,

C14 glass, St. Blaise, Halam

Fledborough, probably has the most early glass, C14 and delightful in pale colours. It is an out of the way church with other treasures to be found in its fabric and monuments.

There is much good Victorian glass, with most of the best designers and makers well represented across the churches in the county. Burne-Jones in High Pavement Chapel, Nottingham (now The Lace Museum) and at St John's, Whatton, colourful glass by Ford Madox Brown in Collingham - Morris and Co, John Hardman, Clayton and Bell at St Mary's, Nottingham. Charles Kempe at Clayworth. St. Barnabas's Roman Catholic Cathedral, Nottingham, has twenty six windows designed by Pugin and made by William Wailes. St Swithun's at East Retford has a wide collection of mid-Victorian windows by well known makers. All Saints', Coddington, has windows by Morris and Ford Madox Brown. Especially memorable are the twenty five windows of 1883-90 in St. Mary Magdalene's, Hucknall by Charles Kempe in his best early period. A brightly coloured window in St. Wilfrid's, Wilford, executed by O'Connor, commemorates the young Nottingham poet Henry Kirke White (1785-1806) who died at only 21, cut short in early promise. He found inspiration in the meadows by the River Trent at Wilford and Clifton, his youthful poetry encouraged by his contemporaries Byron and Southey.

All Saints', Babworth has a rare survival of very late Georgian glass, a Resurrection window of 1830 by Francis Eginton - elegant in the "painters in oil" character of the period. Modern glass of distinction is in All Saints', Misterton with a window of 1965 designed by the distinguished painter John Piper and made by Patrick Reyntiens. There is an interesting window in the north aisle of St. Mary the Virgin, Plumtree, a memorial window by Christine Bodicombe in modern idiom but made in the manner of the C12. She was a pupil of both John Piper and Patrick Reyntiens, but her talents were tragically lost in 1968 when she died only 28 years old. In The Good Shepherd, the Roman Catholic church (1963-6) at Arnold, Patrick Reyntiens achieves a wonderfully brilliant display with slab glass joined by concrete in dalle-de-verre technique.

monuments

Funerary monuments are important elements in the character of churches and a valuable part of our cultural heritage. Not only are they memorials to the deceased, they can also be important works of creative art, essential archives of history, customs, religious and social attitudes.

Monuments in all forms can be found in Nottinghamshire churches. One of the earliest is in St. Andrew's, Skegby, it is the figure of a warden of Sherwood Forest carrying his horn, and alongside, his wife in wimple and gown, of around 1300. A lady of the same period in a wimple, at prayer with a dog at her feet lies in St. Lawrence's, Norwell. A monument to another forest officer, Thomas Leake, a Ranger killed in 1598, is in the delightful church of St. Mary's, Blidworth, rebuilt in 1739.

Mediaeval and Tudor period carved alabaster effigies and tomb chests survive in many churches - notable early ones in Strelley, Clifton and Willoughby-on-the-Wolds churches, to the families of those names. There are Sacheverells to be found in Ratcliffe-on-Soar and in Barton-in-Fabis. There are fine late period memorials to Archbishop Sandys (1588) in Southwell Minster, to Edward Burnell (1590) in St Peter's, Sibthorpe and to Lord Scroope in St Andrews, Langar (1609). In the crypt at Newstead Abbey is a table tomb of alabaster to Sir John Byron of Colwick Hall, who acquired the remains of the dissolved Priory in 1540. Also a splendid rich monument to his son "Little Sir John with great beard," d.1604 and his wife, in Jacobean style. These monuments were brought here in 1937 when Colwick church was abandoned. Their descendant the eminent poet George Gordon the 6th Lord Byron, died in Greece in 1824 and is buried in the Byron family vault in Hucknall church.

Probably the most extraordinary monument in the county is that erected by Anthony Babington in 1540 in St. Winifred's, Kingston-on-Soar. It has a large pillared canopy, is embattled and pinnacled and is carved all over with devices - lozenges and babes in tuns (a play on Babington). The chantry is not particularly refined but is remarkably robust - it dominates the church interior and is probably without parallel.

In St Mary's, Staunton-in-the-Vale are Staunton knights in chain mail from the C13 and C14 - with their ladies, and other later monuments of Nottinghamshire's oldest family, their name going back directly to 1041.

An unusual memorial is the C14 oak effigy to Adam Everingham's (d.1341) second wife, but with his first wife lying alongside him in stone. This is the only wooden effigy in a Nottinghamshire church.

Detail of Babington Monument, Kingston-on-Soar.

Church brasses were made of latten, an alloy of copper and tin imported from Flanders and introduced in the early C13. They were popular for monuments for the lesser gentry and merchants. A few good mediaeval memorial brasses survive. Those at Strelley, Wollaton and East Markham churches are interesting, the latter one to Dame Millicent Meryng (1419) is large and very good. In St. Mary's, Clifton is Sir Robert Clifton (1478) in his armour, and nearby his son Sir Gervase. There are delightful brasses in St Giles's, Darlton, probably to Sir William Meryng and his wife.

There is a vestmented priest on a brass (c.1400) in St John the Baptist's, Stanford-on-Soar, one of only two brasses to clerics in the county - the other is to Ralph Babington in St Luke's, Hickling, the Rector who died in 1521.

The one in The Church of the Holy Rood, Ossington is notable for being a palimpsest - a turned and re-cut brass. The most splendid one is the great brass of the 1360's to Alan Fleming in St. Mary Magdalene's, Newark. Another notable later monument is the one carved in stone to Anne Markham (1601) from the disused church of St Michael's at Cotham and now in St. Mary Magdalene's, Newark. There is the splendid high tiered one of 1602, in the Holy Rood, Ossington, with William Cartwright kneeling in armour, facing his wife. Below on the lower tier are the free standing mourning figures of six sons and six daughters. There are Lexingtons (1723) in St. Wilfrid's, Kelham, Molyneux at St Catherine's, Teversal and the extraordinary Sir Thomas Parkyns in wrestling pose in St Mary's, Bunny. Elegant marble figures of the two Denison brothers (1783) carved by the fashionable sculptor Joseph Nollekens, stand on their plinths in the Holy Rood, Ossington. An early standing figure of Dame Frances Earle c.1687 is in St. Peter's and St .Paul, Sturton-le-Steeple. There are figures in the semi-reclining pose of the period - one to William Huntingdon of 1722, a shipwright, in the little classical brick church of St. Mary's at West Stockwith, built beside the River Trent by his executors. A more grandiose affair is the memorial to Edward Mellish of 1703 in St Mary's and St Martin's at Blyth.

Three wall monuments in the chancel at St. Mary Magdalene's, Newark have lifelike painted busts of C17 worthies set in classical frames.

There is representative work of all the great sculptors of the C18 and C19 - Nollekens, Roubilliac, Flaxman, Westmacott and Chantrey in Nottinghamshire churches. None of these monuments are exceptional in a national context, but worth seeking out for their individuality.

South Nottinghamshire churchyards adjacent to the Vale of Belvoir are notable for their early and attractive Swithland slate headstones. They date from 1700 and their great feature is the fine engraving - the earliest are in delightful free primitive form. The later C18 and very early C19 ones are in elegant penman script with flourishes. Due to the hardness of the slate these engravings have survived the elements so much better than those cut in other stones.

Many fine examples exist in Hickling, Granby, Lowdham, Saundby, Ratcliffe-on-Trent and Stanford-on-Soar churchyards amongst others.

William Huntingdon monument, West Stockwith

At St Winifred, Holbeck is a tablet to Major Lord William Augustus Cavendish - Bentinck of Welbeck (d.1902) and a tombstone to Lady Ottoline Morrell (d.1938) carved by the unconventional but gifted sculptor and letterer Eric Gill. Lady Ottoline Morrell (née Bentinck) was half sister of the 6th Duke of Portland - William Arthur Bentinck - she was a leading figure in the intellectual and aesthetic "Bloomsbury Set" of the early C20 and a gifted patron of numerous writers, poets and painters of the period, including Nottinghamshire's D. H. Lawrence (see also Cossall) - who rather unkindly repaid her friendships with an unflattering portrayal of her in his novel "Women in Love".

But, perhaps the most remarkable memorial survival in the county is the Saxon coffin lid in St Luke's, Hickling, with a carved cross, a riot of interlaced knotwork, and animals also included. A unique example of a Saxon coped tombstone.

Detail of carved Saxon coffin lid, Hickling

NOTTINGHAMSHIRE ALABASTERS

The earliest surviving alabaster tomb figure is of c.1300 in Hanbury church near Tutbury, Staffordshire. The hill there was one of the earliest sources of the material.

Alabaster is a rare type of gypsum mineral in compacted form. It can be finely carved, and after exposure to air it hardens and can then be polished to a marble like finish. It is slightly translucent, but takes coloured paint and gilding, attributes important to mediaeval work.

Swithland slate headstone, Hickling

Gypsum is now mined largely to make plaster. It occurs in strata close to the surface in a band near the line of the River Trent from Tutbury, Staffordshire through South Derbyshire and up through Nottinghamshire. Workable alabaster occurred as nodules above the main gypsum beds - principally only at Tutbury, Chellaston Hill, Derbyshire and Red Hill, Ratcliffe-on-Soar, Nottinghamshire, all are now essentially worked out. In mediaeval times alabaster came almost wholly from the first two sources since they produced the white or mainly colourless form then in prime demand. Red veined alabaster from Red Hill only became more acceptable after the white began to run out in the mid 1500s. A good example of the Red Hill is probably Archbishop Sandys (died 1588) tomb in Southwell Minster, and certainly the twenty huge alabaster columns each 25 feet high in Kedleston Hall, Derbyshire from the Curzon family's own quarry at Ratcliffe-on-Soar.

The principal mediaeval centre for carving chest tombs and effigies became established in Chellaston alongside the alabaster pits. But the main place for carving figure panels for altar pieces, standing figures and small devotional plaques of St John the Baptist was in Nottingham largely using Chellaston alabaster. The trade became considerable with demand all over England and on mainland Europe. Nottingham 'alablasterers' or 'imagemakers' were well established when Edward III commissioned a large alabaster altar piece for the Chapel of St George, Windsor in 1367. Early standing figures were mainly 'flat backs' and remarkable surviving examples are three figures from c.1380 of the Virgin, St Peter, and a Bishop, found at the demolished Church of St Peter, Flawford near Ruddington (now in the Castle Museum, Nottingham).

From the mid 1400s, altar pieces came to consist of five or seven carved biblical scenes flanked by saints, all set in a carved oak frame in the form of a hinged triptych. The carvings and frame were painted in rich polychrome and gilding. Larger wall mounted reredos were made, but most were of the smaller type to stand on the altars - probably because they were more easily transported from Nottingham. Some were sent as far away as Iceland and Norway. None now survive in English churches in original form (the only complete one is in the Victoria and Albert Museum). There are some 34 complete or near complete English alabaster altar pieces still in Continental churches, and over three thousand panels or major parts survive there - most no doubt the Nottingham 'alablasters' work. How many were exported before the Reformation and how many re-sold there when cleared from English churches is indeterminate. All English altar pieces and figures were swept away by an Act of Edward VI in 1550 which abolished the use of missals in church, and demanded the destruction of all religious images - alabaster ones being specifically mentioned. Thousands were destroyed, others sold abroad, and some hidden away buried like the three Flawford figures. The Nottingham industry collapsed after this statute was decreed.

Pieces of panel have been found under other church floors, including a C15 one from under the sanctuary in St Mary's, Nottingham - from the heart of the 'alablastermen's' industry - it is now displayed in the chapel to the south of the chancel. A poorly preserved panel of the Trinity can be seen in St John the Evangelists', Carlton-in-Lindrick.

There is an extensive collection of these alabaster

panels to be seen in the Castle Museum, Nottingham, including the Flawford figures.

CHURCHYARDS

The origins of churchyards are not wholly clear but seem to derive from several precedents. First mention of the consecration of a churchyard is in the sixth century. Their establishment in England is confirmed in 752 when the Archbishop of Canterbury obtained the Pope's consent for their establishment in towns. The more precise statement of the acre (God's acre) was defined in 943, but as late as the C14 churchyards still had no legal recognition. Acts of conservation necessitated that the area should have its boundaries defined. In 1229 the Bishop of Worcester ordered that churchyards should be enclosed by wall, hedge or ditch. These defined boundaries were generally of a square or rectangular shape. Churchyards of circular shape are rare and often an indication that the site was originally pagan. The churchyard at Holy Trinity, Wysall is circular and is therefore likely to be of considerable age.

The diversity of character between churchyards is an individual joy. Some are well endowed with trees and others quite open. Despite the legend about churchyard yews and the use of their boughs for bows, they were more likely planted for windbreak and shade. Some churchyards are raised substantially above the surrounding ground through centuries of burials. A few churches have lychgates, literally 'corpse-gate.' These were provided as a sheltered resting place for the coffin and corpse when they had to be carried or conveyed on a cart from a distance, before entry into church. The priest would meet the mourners there and start the opening sentences of the burial service. All Saints', Bingham has a lychgate - there is another tiny token one at St Nicholas's, Littleborough. A very unusual one can be seen at St George's, North and South Clifton all in iron with a barrel roof, incorporated lettered texts, and large iron gates matching the adjacent iron railings.

In St Helen's churchyard, Stapleford is the tall shaft of a pre-Norman cross c.1050, with interlacing decoration - the most important early monument in the county. At St Mary's and All Saints', Hawksworth are the remains of a Saxon cross about 6 feet tall with interlace and crosses. Both these are probably the remains of church preaching crosses.

Saxon cross shaft, Stapleford

In mediaeval times churchyards were used for community purposes since there was rarely other available space. Village fairs were held in the churchyard, as were sports including wrestling (see St Mary's, Bunny and Sir Thomas Parkyns), ball games, archery practice and Church-Ales, which were fund raising efforts like latter day bazaars and church teas. Headstones are a comparatively recent introduction from the late C17 and therefore did not obstruct the open space in earlier time. Graves were originally grouped around the churchyard cross, usually in a southern position. The north side of the church was generally shunned for burial from the C17 to C19 and thought only suitable for burial of unbaptized infants, strangers, paupers and suicides.

Two of the earliest headstones in the county are at St Catherine's, Teversal - plain low stones, one dated 1631. Many C18 headstones are works of art. The exceptional collection in Nottinghamshire are the Swithland slate ones in the Vale of Belvoir churchyards. Early primitive ones delight with their lack of symmetry in the setting out of the lettering and in relief deriving from wood carving technique. A good example of this form is the headstone to Richard Attonbrow (d.1728) in the churchyard of St. Mary's, Clifton, Nottingham. These are followed by inscribed ones still following the asymmetrical layout - then there are balanced designs with lettering in penmanship style with elegant flourishes. Most of the early ones have cherubs at the head with triangular wings. After about 1720 many of these stones are signed by their makers. Of these, James Sparrow of Radcliffe-on-Trent was probably the most prolific and accomplished.

NONCONFORMIST CHAPELS AND MEETING HOUSES

The county holds an important place in the early history of nonconformity, beginning with the Independent Church formed at Scrooby in the early C17. Mansfield played a significant part in the early difficult years of the Society of Friends. Nottingham was the scene of some early Methodist activity. Early meeting houses and chapels are largely disappointing and few continue in their original use. Many have been demolished in comparatively recent years. Other once significant ones in Nottingham and elsewhere have been so altered that in their converted uses they bear little resemblance externally, let alone internally, to their original character. Most villages still have their red brick early chapels, long altered to other use, but still bearing their date tablets.

Among interesting survivors are - The Wesleyan Chapel, Barnby Gate, Newark opened in 1846, Kirkby Woodhouse General Baptist, built in

The Wesleyan Chapel, Barnby Gate, Newark

1754, altered and heightened 1865-66; Cropwell Bishop Wesleyan of 1842; Methodist Church, Wellow of 1840, in a particularly delightful setting; East Leake General Baptist built 1756, altered/heightened in 1839; the Wesleyan Chapel, Clayworth of 1834. Southwell Baptists have occupied their building since 1839, but it was originally built as a workhouse in c.1800.

The Old Meeting House, Stockwell Gate, Mansfield is probably the oldest surviving nonconformist chapel in the county and was built by the Unitarians in 1702. The door entrances were altered in 1870, followed in 1882 by the addition of a chancel, organ chamber and vestry. This, with the re-orientation of the seating changed the layout into a mediaeval church tradition.

Perhaps the most dominant chapel in the county is the former High Pavement Chapel in Nottingham which is now a Lace Museum. The Presbyterian Society, latterly Unitarian, built its first church on this site in 1690-91. It was replaced in 1804-05 with a new building of plain rectangular shape, again being replaced in 1874-76 by the present ambitious building. Built in a mixture of Gothic style, it is prominent through its tall tower, corner pinnacles, spire, and siting on the edge of the Lace Market cliff. The exterior has no outstanding architectural merits, but the interior is more rewarding with a good east window portraying 21 figures of virtues and learning - made by Morris and Co in 1890 to the design of Burne-Jones.

The Lace Hall, Nottingham

ELIGIOUS FIGURES

Nottinghamshire churches have connections with a number of notable religious figures who left their individual imprints on history.

Thomas Cranmer, first Protestant Archbishop of Canterbury, was born in 1489 in the Manor House at Aslockton and attended Whatton church in his childhood, where his father's memorial survives. Cranmer annulled Henry VIII's marriage to Catherine of Aragon. Under Edward VI he advanced the Reformation and compiled the Anglican

'Book of Common Prayer.' In the subsequent short reign of Mary I he was found guilty of heresy, condemned as a traitor and burnt at the stake in Oxford.

Also well known were William Brewster (b.1566) and William Bradford (b.1590) who founded the Scrooby Separatist Church and subsequently sailed in 'The Mayflower' to establish Plymouth Colony in New England, America - two of the original Pilgrim Fathers. Coupled with these men is the Rev. Clifton of Babworth, the free thinker who inspired Brewster and Bradford by his preachings against the rituals of the established Church of England.

George Fox (b.1624) was a Nottingham shoemaker's apprentice who established the Society of Friends (the Quakers), and spread their beliefs through England, and in journeys to Holland and America.

John Wesley (b.1703) was born at Epworth just outside the county. From beginnings as an Anglican priest he became an Evangelist. His early preaching tours included north Nottinghamshire villages like Misterton, and the town of East Retford where he held open air meetings. In 1729 he founded the Methodist Movement.

William Booth was born at Sneinton, Nottingham in 1829. His birthplace has been restored and become a small museum. At the age of 17 he became a passionate Methodist preacher. But eventually he tired of its restraints and passed to independent evangelic work. From missionary work among the poor in London he founded the Salvation Army in 1878 as a Christian social movement.

INCLUDED CHURCHES

			page
St Nicholas	Littleborough	X	22
St Mary and St Martin	Blyth		23
St Mary the Virgin	Southwell Minster		26
Our Lady and St Cuthbert	Worksop	+	32
St Mary	East Leake		36
St Mary	Bunny		38
St Mary	Edwinstowe		41
All Saints	Hawton	X	43
St Mary Magdalene	Newark		46
St Mary the Virgin	Nottingham		50
All Saints	Babworth	X	52
St Wilfrid	Scrooby	X	55
St Catherine	Teversal	X	58
The Holy Rood	Ossington	X	60
St Catherine	Cossall	X	62
St Barnabas RC Cathedral	Nottingham		63

X Churches so marked are normally kept locked outside service times, against the risks of vandals. Some have notices saying where the key is held. Rectors, Vicars, Priests in Charge will generally be pleased to help genuine visitors.

+ Worksop Priory is normally only open additionally to services, on Monday, Wednesday and Friday mornings.

LITTLEBOROUGH
St Nicholas

A gem of a church set in a remote part of the countryside. Today the village is a hamlet of only two or three houses alongside the River Trent, with Lincolnshire on the other bank. Although now a wonderfully quiet spot, it was in Roman times an important place, the site of the fort and township of Segelocum at the ferry and ford crossing of the road from Lincoln across to Doncaster. In the C18 the road, as the route from Retford to Lincoln, was turnpiked and served by a chain ferry, continuing in use well into the

Littleborough, the tiny Norman Church.

present century. Importance has long gone with the building of bridge crossings elsewhere and abandonment of the ferry. A hexagonal tollhouse survives nearby at the Cottam road junction - a rare survivor in the county.

The church is a tiny Norman building of nave and chancel. The north side is unfortunately marred by a tacked-on brick vestry. Entry into the church is by doors set in a rather plain Norman arch in the west end, flanked by a pair of substantial buttresses. Above on this gable is a bellcote with two bells. Although remade at some time the bellcote is probably of near original appearance. The bells are of especial interest, one being the oldest known in the county. The sanctus bell dates from around 1200, and the other from 1350. It is possible that they were cast in the Nottingham bell foundry.

Interior, Littleborough Church.

Detail of east window, Littleborough.

The external walls in random laid blue lias have extensive areas of typical Norman herringbone pattern stonework. Also incorporated are reused fragments of Roman brick. The nave windows and chancel east window are C19 ones, though of Romanesque character. The stained glass in the east window dates from 1900. The chancel south side window still has its original deep splays, and its size is probably the original pattern for the building.

Inside, the most individual feature of the church is the chancel arch with roll moulding, supported by narrow attached pillars with primitively carved 'palm leaf' heads. Set in the south wall of the chancel is a piscina of Early English form, late C12 or early C13 with typical nailhead ornament, and a carved face below. The altar rails are pleasing with turned oak balusters. Plain C19 pews fill the nave and an ancient tiny organ is also squeezed in. Just inside the door is an old plain round font with an early C18, Queen Anne period cover.

The surrounding churchyard is equally tiny, with well worn headstones in the grass, and a small timbered lychgate completing the peaceful setting in the open landscape.

BLYTH St Mary and St Martin

The approach through Blyth and the view up the churchyard approach is dominated by the great Perpendicular west tower. This with the stately early Decorated period south aisle give no inkling of what is to be seen within. It is only when we enter that the remains of a great nave

Blyth Church.

and its north aisle come into view. This early Norman work in awesome severity is similar in character to its precedent, the great Abbey church of Notre Dame at Jumièges near Rouen, France - dedicated in 1067.

Blyth church was originally part of the Benedictine Priory founded in 1088 by Roger de Builli of Tickhill Castle; the first mediaeval monastery to be established in Nottinghamshire. Through its position on the major route to the north and with its fairs and markets, Blyth became an important town in mediaeval times. The Priory was a convenient place of hospitality for travellers, and through its rights of toll and endowments it became enriched.

The Priory was originally subordinate to the Abbey of St Catherine at Rouen. The plan layout with apsidal chancel and straight-ended chapels alongside reflected Normandy precedents such as Bernay Abbey. Building started very soon after foundation, probably as was customary from the chancel end, but with such speed that the whole including the nave was finished by about 1100.

The nave was originally of seven bays. Then there was the crossing, no doubt with a short tower, with the apsidal chancel beyond. Alongside were two square ended chapels, with further flanking apsidal ended chapels in parallel. There are three elements to the nave walls - the arcade, a gallery triforium and the clerestory above. The piers of the nave are square masonry with half shafts on the face running up to the roof. From these spring the thin graceful ribs of the vaulted roof inserted in about 1230. The shafts would originally have run right up to the roof which would have been a flat timber one above the clerestory. There are demi-columns on the insides of the piers of the arcade with simple capitals decorated only with rudimentary corner volutes. The two carved heads on the second capital from the east on the north are thought to represent the founder and his wife. The arches of the gallery are plain and rise with hardly a break from the arcade.

The north aisle is as original, spare with its small round headed windows and bare groined roof with transverse arches.

Early Norman south arcade, Blyth.

The south aisle would have been similar but in about 1290 it was taken down and the wider stately aisle that we now see was built. Externally this is of a regular seven bays divided with stepped buttresses. In five bays are wide pointed windows with simple three light intersecting tracery. Above is a regular battlemented parapet with projecting gargoyles along the string course, aligned above each buttress. The westernmost bay has no window but a small round headed Norman doorway gives everyday entrance to the church. The roomy south porch in Early English style has two orders at its entrance, a well moulded pointed arch and decorated capitals. The battlemented parapet is identical to that on the aisle, with more winged gargoyles - but additionally has slender crocketted pinnacles. There is reason to think that the aisle also originally had similar pinnacles along the bays. The wall stonework of the porch is however different from the aisle wall. It has been suggested that this is an earlier C13 porch rebuilt in its new position when the present aisle was built. Inside the porch are wide bench seats and the roof has moulded beams with foliated bosses. Note the smiling face on the beam above the inner doorway.

Carved stone boss to nave vault, Blyth, c.1230.

It is reputed that in the late C14 there were disputes between the townspeople and the Priory. This may be the cause for the building in around 1400 of the great end wall across the nave at the first bay. Although why at this position is curious, since the entry to the chancel was the more usual division between clerics and laiety. That the wall is certainly of this date and not later is evidenced by the great Doom Painting, now cleaned of its centuries' coating of lime wash. It was known that there was some painting on this wall but it wasn't until cleaning began in 1987 as part of the Nine Centuries Celebrations of the church, that the full extent became revealed. The Doom is a portrayal of the Day of Judgement, with visions of those going to heaven, and sinners down to hell.

The great west tower also dates from around 1400. Stately but simple, relieved only by the elegant arched links to the battlements, and decorated with crockets like the eight pinnacles. It is a statement of the townspeople's pride and may, like the wall, have been their reply to disputes. The delightful west doorway to the tower is elaborated with bold leaved crockets rising to a central finial with a gabled hood mould above. The sides of the doorway are framed with attached slender pannelled pinnacles, also crocketted - and adjacent are plunging dolphins.

The tower completely replaces the Norman west end. It is impossible to say now what that was like, but reasonable conjecture is that it would have had twin towers capped with pyramidal roofs flanking a gable ended nave with a central main entrance doorway. There are now no remains of the east end. The whole of the chancel, side chapels, crossing and transepts were pulled down after the Dissolution in 1535 when the Priory buildings were sold. Blyth Hall was eventually built on the site of the Priory's domestic buildings, that is on the north side of the church. The last hall on the site, the seat of the Mellish family, built in 1685, was demolished in 1972 and built over with houses. In consequence of the wall across the nave, this left the old end bay of the nave curiously outside, open to the elements. The modern facing and shaping of this east end has given it a rather surprising baroque form.

In the C18 the interior was filled with galleries and box pews, but these were all removed in 1885. The south aisle is set out as the parish church with the old nave and north aisle left clear for public space. There is a contemporary C15 screen across the south aisle, vaulted on both sides, and with painted figures of saints in the bottom panels. St Stephen, St Edmund, St Euphemia, St Helena, St Barbara, St Ursula. In some respects similar to several Norfolk and Suffolk painted screens. The rood screen across the nave is in poorer state, but also bears traces of painted saints. There is a parclose screen between nave and aisle. In addition to the painted Doom there is remaining mediaeval wall paint with jointing picked out, on the pillar behind the altar - also faint traces of paint on the upper walls in the nave. Curiously, similar traces of wall paint survives at Jumièges Abbey.

The font is late C17 with cherub's heads - William & Mary Period - as is the cover.
The pulpit is early C17. There is wall panelling that comes from some of the old box pews, and backs and ends of present pews also come from this source.

There are a few monuments. A plaque arranged across one of the piers has pilaster framing with a cherub below over crossed sword and anchor, all topped with an elegant urn with swags, to Thomas Hudson - a merchant and his wife of c.1772. A large memorial to Edward Mellish d.1702, of Blyth Hall, rather stiffly reclining, framed with Corinthian pilasters and segmental pediment above with urns - moderately good, but interesting because of being the earliest figure in such a pose in a Nottinghamshire church. There is a damaged effigy of a knight c.1240 - thought to be a Fitzwilliam, and three grave slabs with foliated crosses stand against the wall under the tower - probably C13 and C14. Five splendid recently restored hatchments of the Mellish family are on the walls.

Blyth is additionally interesting for its dual dedication. Clearly the Priory Church was St Mary's. Was St Martin a dedication from an earlier church or, from one of the now lost chapels or, did the parish church take this dedication when it was separated by the wall in c.1400?

SOUTHWELL MINSTER
St. Mary The Virgin

The great church dominates the delightful little town. There are glimpses of the Minster from a distance on the approaches, but one is still startled by its sudden presence. If anything, the Westgate approach is the more awe-inspiring with the view of the great west towers soaring upward, capped with steep pyramidal roofs quite unlike anywhere else in England.

The church's known origins are in a grant of the Manor of Southwell by King Eadwig to Oskytel, Archbishop of York in 956. It is presumed a Saxon church was built soon after since it is known the remains of St Eadburgh were interred here early in C11. The extent of the Saxon church is unknown but it no doubt lay within the site of the present church. In the south transept can be seen beneath the floor a section of Roman floor mosaic. It is known that the remains of a Roman Villa lies beyond the east end of the church (a section of its painted wall plaster is on display in the south choir) and it is possible the tesserae were re-used in the Saxon church.

The church at Southwell from its earliest days was established as collegiate. A minster church was where the priests were secular canons and

Southwell Minster from the north-west.

not monks of a closed order such as the Benedictines. Their obligations were maintenance of services in their church, care of the fabric and the spiritual care of souls. They were supported by income from endowments of property and tithes known as prebends (or providers) and the priests were accordingly known as Prebendaries. There were probably 7 canons at first, rising to 16 by the late C13. The system was not unique to Southwell - York, Lincoln and others were incorporated in this way. By the time of the Norman Conquest in 1066 the college was well established. The canons had land and their houses around the Minster garth; later rebuilds of these can be seen. Because of their dual duties of minster and separate parish priests, the Prebendaries in fairly early days appointed Vicars Choral and Vicars Parochial to act in their absence in the Minster, and in their parish churches. The collegiate form continued, apart from a short break between 1547 and restoration by Queen Elizabeth in 1585, until final cessation in 1841. Southwell had acted as the mother church of Nottinghamshire with responsibility for the southern part of the great Diocese of York from 1108. The Archbishops made regular Visitations and stayed in the adjacent Bishop's Palace. Six Archbishops died there and were buried in the Minster, although the only known tomb now is that of Archbishop Sandys d.1588 (see also the ledger stone of his grand-daughter Penelope Sandys in Scrooby Church). Southwell with some 25 parishes in the county became a Peculiar, a separate ecclesiastical district run by the chapter of canons, outside and exempt from control of the Archdeaconry of Nottingham. From 1841 it remained only as a parish church until made a cathedral of the new Diocese of Southwell, including Derbyshire as well as Nottinghamshire until 1927. This is why there are still named seats for Derbyshire canons in the chapter house.

The present church is of three main building periods - comprising the nave, choir and chapter house. The Normans began to rebuild the Saxon church after 1108 when Archbishop Thomas of

York raised its status to the mother church and encouraged rebuilding and enlargement. The nave, aisles, transepts, towers and north porch are from this great rebuild. The choir of that date was less than half the length we see now, with a square end but apsidal ended choir aisles. There were also chapels in the ends of the transepts with apsidal ends on the east side. These apses were later removed, but the apse opening arches can still be seen. The choir was taken down and rebuilt in 1234-41 and the chapter house added from 1288.

The nave is of seven bays plus an extra short one between the west towers. The arcade is of circular piers on square bases, and simple round capitals decorated with minimal shallow scalloping patterns in variety. The arches have billet moulding to the outside with double rolls to their soffites. Above is a string course, enlivened with chevron moulding, on which stands the triforium. Here the arches repeat the form and decoration of the arcade, but are supported on short attached half columns with scalloped block capitals. Stumps within the arch soffites suggest it was originally intended to sub-divide the openings but for some unknown reason this was abandonded.

Chapter house doorway, Southwell.

The clerestory is largely blank wall with plain round headed openings to the gallery behind.

We see the interior facades rolling onward without interruption, drawing eyes eastward. Henry Thorold imaginatively suggests it is an effect not unlike the arches of a great Roman aqueduct such as that at Pont du Gard, Nimes, France. Comparison should be made between the austerity of Blyth, the restlessness of Worksop and the maturity of Southwell.

The waggon-ribbed roof is a replacement of 1800 but it complements the character of the nave admirably. The aisles have ribbed vaults, not yet fully developed but no longer primitive as at Blyth. Also the aisle windows are now much larger than at Blyth. Only the north east one is original, the others are renewed replicas. The aisle windows in the four easternmost bays each side are enlarged replacements of the C15 in the Perpendicular style.

Pulpitum detail, Southwell, C1340.

Along the walls of the aisles are the original low stone bench seating.

The crossing is impressive with tall half round columns to the transepts' arches, rising to half-way up the triforium, and again there is a shallow scalloped fringe to the capitals. The nave and choir piers of the crossing have composite columns, but are more specifically important for their carved capitals. The eastern pair have small corner volutes and pictorial representations

Rare Norman historiated capital, Southwell, C1120. The Annunciation.

of the Last Supper, the Annunciation, Entry into Jerusalem, the Agnus Dei, and the Washing of Feet - executed like manuscript drawings, the people carved with great staring eyes. The arches above are elaborated with cable and wave decoration on the rolls. The transepts are strong and restrained. There is some arcading to the lowest stage of windows. The triforium and clerestory stages above also have round headed windows, each with a single order of relief columns supporting cable moulding and plain arch respectively. Surprisingly the clerestory windows show as circular ones to the outside. Above the former apse arches in the east wall of each transept, three bay arcaded galleries break the rhythm of the window pattern on the adjacent walls. Behind the window piercings of the clerestory stage is a narrow wall passage.

Externally, the twin towers are original and now unique in England. They are typical of what would have been seen on many great Norman churches. To complete the picture we have to imagine the central crossing tower would also originally have had a pyramidal roof. Worksop Priory is the only other surviving example of twin towers but now without pyramids and with later added crenellated parapets. The pyramids on the west towers at Southwell are replicas put on in 1880 to restore them to their pre-1711 appearance, after they, the nave and tower roofs were destroyed by fire. The towers have shallow corner buttresses, and are divided by string courses into six stages. At the sixth stage is blank arcading carried all round. The intersections forming narrow pointed arches, a presage of the future Gothic style.

The west doorway has four orders of columns with zig-zag moulding to the arches, enclosing splendid original C12 doors with scrolly ironwork. The great Perpendicular style west window inserted in the C15, with crenellated parapet above, is a fine example but unfortunately radically altered the original form of the west front.

Along the sides of the aisles is a string course of zig-zag pattern, broken and taken down below the late C14 windows when these were altered. An eaves band runs along at the edges of the nave and aisles roofs, the bottom decorated with spaced scallops. Clerestory windows are circular, and surrounded with a frame. There is a fine large Norman porch on the north side, with a handsome arch supported on two orders of half round columns. The porch is two storey with a trio of windows in the gable, ornamented with zig-zag, cable and grotesques, lighting the upper room - originally for the Sacristan. At the corners are round pinnacles - one perforated but otherwise disguising its use as the chimney for the fireplace inside. Along the sides the eaves bands are supported on a row of heads. Inside, the porch has a plain tunnel vault rising off an intersecting blank arcade along each side - its colonnettes resting on the side stone benching. The inner doorway is very fine, with five orders, scalloped cushion capitals and arches decorated with several forms of zig-zag ornament and one with beakhead. The later C14 door is coffered all over with ogee patterns. The porch is a fine composition and a remarkable survival for its date.

The transepts have flat buttresses and pilasters and are horizontally divided with string courses. Windows have single orders and zig-zag ornament to the arches. Clerestory windows are again roundels, and the gable ends are sumptuously decorated with diapered zig-zag and rows of dotted holes.

The great central tower is splendid Norman work. The two upper stages have blank arcading, which is particularly lively on the lower where it is of intersecting form matching the west towers. The plain parapet has a scalloped lower edge, with circular corner pinnacles and shorter intermediate ones. The south side corner pinnacles have diaper and dot pattern like the transept gables.

Early in the C13 it was decided that the choir space was inadequate for the growing body of clergy and choristers. In 1234 Archbishop Walter de Gray gave stimulus to the work of replacing the Norman choir with a new one in the latest style. This beautifully balanced example of Early English Gothic, completed in 1250 is what we see today. The choir was doubled in length and its side aisles extended, all finished with square ends. On the sides are two small chapels projecting like mini-transepts. The internal elevations of the choir are arranged to appear in two tiers. The arcade has piers of four major and four minor filleted shafts with deep hollows between. Moulded capitals have minimal nailhead ornament and there are multi-moulded pointed arches. Above is a tall order of twin lancets to each bay with a gallery and plain lancet windows in pairs to the set back clerestory. The roof has ribbed quadripartite vaulting. In the sanctuary, the two end bays and the east wall window run round as continuous lancets, with clustered colonnettes between - their capitals carved with stiff leaf foliage. Bold dog tooth ornament runs round their multi-moulded arches. The whole a superb composition in classic Early English style. In the south choir aisle is a later C15 doorway, now blocked, ornamented with label stop heads of an unidentified King and Queen. (These may be Henry III and Queen Eleanor during whose reign the choir was built - there is a resemblance to his effigy in Westminster Abbey). In the side chapels are built-in arcaded seating and piscinas. Externally the choir is much plainer, with the paired lancets relieved with one order of colonnettes, intervening buttresses with strong gabled tops and a bold multi-moulded plinth. Along the clerestory parapet is a corbel course of many heads with an infinite variety of faces. The flying buttresses and pinnacles to the clerestory are later, early C14 and probably relate to the removal of the original steep pitched roofs to the choir side chapels.

In the late 1260s the Norman apse chapel in the north transept was taken down and replaced with the present vaulted chapel of two equal bays. This present Pilgrim's Chapel may originally have been two chapels. The windows are C14 replacements with geometrical style tracery. It has a chamber over - more recently used as the library.

The final main phase of building was the chapter house which was begun in the late 1280s. In 1288 the new Archbishop John le Romaine came on a Visitation to his palace and while there he issued a decree for the building of a chapter house with a levy on the prebends towards its costs. The chapter house is the supreme glory of the Minster, a masterpiece of mediaeval craftsmanship. Of a regular octagon in plan, it was built contemporarily with the larger one at York Minster. But although smaller, Southwell is distinguished and unique in its daring, having no centre support for the stone ribbed roof - its web of moulded ridge ribs interspersed with intermediate ones, the innovation of tierceron ribs. At the external corners of the building are great buttresses to take the roof thrust, allowing the inclusion of large windows between. Each are three lancet lights, the upper parts of the window filled with geometrical roundels and trefoils, and delicate tracery between. The pierced parapet supported by dropped trefoils terminates in a variety of carved heads, and is divided by pinnacles to the buttresses, intricately decorated with crockets and sub-pinnacles. The exterior of the adjacent vestibule is plainer, but the gabled buttresses are more unusually decorated with large naturalistic heads of beasts - a ram, boar, bull, fish - with more grotesques above. In the building of the chapter house we see the Early English style clearly merging into the next development of Gothic architecture the Decorated style.

Entrance to the chapter house is via a doorway in the choir south aisle, giving on to a short passage lined with a low arcade on colonnettes, the east side with its twin columns was originally open as a small cloister. The passage terminates in high vestibule, then turns at right angles into the chapter house. The elegant entrance arch is divided into two openings with a slender composite column supporting a tracery roundel filled with a quatrefoil. The arch is of four orders and enriched with columns of English Purbeck fossilised marble. The pattern of arcading runs round the chapter house with a continuous row of 36 sedilia each crowned by cusped arches and ornamented gables.

But, the greatest of all the achievements at Southwell is the wonderful relief carved natural foliage in the chapter house, passage and vestibule. Leaves of maple, oak, hawthorn, vine and buttercup. Heads and creatures - a boar, hare and hounds, birds lurk in the foliage which covers all the capitals and on springing label stops. In corners and sudden surprising points are heads and figures in variety - lords, ladies, kings, bishops, clerics, craftsmen, common men and idiots, creatures and mythological forms, such as a merman. In the tympanum above the seating, the green man with head wreathed in leafy stems - Jack in the Green, the May King, Robin Wood (Robin-of-the-Wood, Robin Hood) a fertility symbol so close in spirit to the riot of foliage. It is impossible to do justice to this wonderful work in all its aspects - a visit is essential and greater insight is to be had from Nikolaus Pevsner's 'Leaves of Southwell' and Norman Summer's 'The Chapter House.'

The final outstanding work at Southwell is the pulpitum or stone rood screen c.1320-40 in full Decorated style. Richly crocketted gables with finials and pinnacles, the choir side has six seats, for the archbishop and prebendaries, each with carved misericords to their underside. The nave side has a three arched arcade, recessed behind with little vaults and delightful flying ribs. Added at the same time is the sedilia in the choir, with the unusual number of five seats. The craftsmanship and style is the same as the pulpitum, luxuriant and masterly. These works have much in common with the Easter Sepulchre at Hawton and are probably by the same hands.

The tympanum set in a wall in the north transept does not belong to its present position. It is difficult to relate it to the church. Carved with St Michael and the Dragon, and with David rescuing his flock from the lion it has an Anglo-Saxon 'Urnes' style but is now thought to be later - perhaps late C11 or early C12. But it is a possibility that it could have been a late addition to the previous Saxon church.

The font is dated 1661, octagonal with bands forming panels filled with stylized fleurs-de-lys and roses - similar to many put in Nottinghamshire churches after the Restoration. The brass eagle lectern of c.1510 was found in the lake at Newstead Abbey and given to Southwell in 1805. Only fragments of the mediaeval glass survive, in the chapter house and, in an assembly in a window of the choir south aisle. The four lower panels of glass installed in 1818 in the east window are C16, bought in Paris, from the former Temple church. There is excellent Victorian pictorial glass of c.1850 by O'Connor in the nave aisles. Also later windows by Kempe - good early work of his, in the eastern nave aisles (1875 and 1880). Later work in the south side of the sanctuary of 1898 and the latest of 1907 in the north transept and adjacent chapel. There are only a few monuments of interest, a slab with foliated cross in an arched recess in the north aisle, several early floor slabs nearby with incised crosses - a recumbent headless debased figure of an Archbishop, thought to be c.1450. There is a splendid alabaster tomb chest and effigy of Archbishop Sandys (d.1588) with figures of his family knelt in prayer on the side panel of the chest. There is also a striking memorial to Bishop Ridding of 1907, designed by W. D. Caröe and sculpted by Pomeroy in bronze, kneeling at an alabaster prie-dieu set on a characterised tomb chest.

Outside at the east end of the Minster garth is The Residence, now occupied by the Provost, and four Vicar's Houses. The Residence, built in 1689 replaced the original Hall of the Vicar's Choral. The Vicar's Houses were built in 1779 replacing earlier ones. There were by that date only six Vicars Choral, and of these two lived in the town. In 1785 The Residence was updated and re-fronted.

The chantry priests' lodging, long demolished, was where later buildings stand at the north west corner of the churchyard.

The Bishop's house by W D Caröe of 1909 incorporates an earlier dwelling and is integrated into the old Archbishop's Palace on the south side of the Minster.

WORKSOP SS Cuthbert and Mary

The church was founded as Radford Priory in 1103 on the banks of the little River Ryton, by William de Lovetot, one of the great Norman lords who owned Worksop and other estates in the county. That church, dedicated to St Cuthbert, was much smaller than the present one. As has been found from excavations on site, it was built with three parallel apses to the east end.

West door, Worksop Priory Church, late twelfth century.

The monastic establishment was founded as an order of Augustinian canons. These were an order organised on monastic lines but where all its members were priests - complementary in effect to the secular canons of Southwell Minster - but differing from other orders of monks, where it was unusual for everyone to be fully ordained priests prior to the time of the C14. The Augustinians were popularly known as black canons from the colour of their habits.

The church was rebuilt from 1140 and it is the earliest parts of the present church that are from this date - these being the western towers and front, the nave and the aisles. At this rebuilding, completed sometime circa 1180, the east end had been rebuilt like the great church of Cluny, France with an apse ended choir, straight ended side aisle chapels, and apse endings to chapels in the transepts. About the time of completion, a dedication to St Mary was added to the existing one to St Cuthbert.

Early in the C13 the Norman choir was taken down and replaced with one in the new Early English style. And, in about 1240, the Lady Chapel was added, extending out from the south transept along the choir aisle. It was built by Lady Maud Furnival in memory of her husband Sir Gerard, the 1st Lord Furnival.

In 1539 came the Dissolution of the greater monasteries. The monks were dispersed, the whole of the east end - choir, transepts, crossing and central tower was pulled down. The east end of the nave was walled up, and with its aisles, became the parish church. On the north, the domestic buildings of the Priory and the chapter house were abandoned. The fabric was carted away for re-use elsewhere. Only three walls of the Lady Chapel were left, isolated and roofless. Miraculously, the magnificent gatehouse to the Priory, on the southern boundary, was permitted to survive.

The Lady Chapel may have been saved from complete demolition because of the burials within of ancestors of noble families - notably Lady Maud Furnival 1st Countess of Shrewsbury who had the chapel built - Sir William Furnival (d.1369) - John Talbot, 2nd Earl of Shrewsbury (d.1460) - John Talbot 3rd Earl of Shrewsbury and Talbot (d.1473).

In 1922 the Lady Chapel was re-roofed and restored by Harold Brakespear. This was followed by re-building in 1929 a linking south transept in a convincing C13 style, then by re-building the crossing, and a north transept in Early English form in 1932. Following a large bequest in 1965, a fund was launched which culminated in the building of a new central tower, a short choir with vestries and sacristy beyond. The visual effect of this latter work has been controversial. The simplicity of the interior and the external massing accord with the earlier C20 work, but the external detail is disappointing.

The general approach to the church today is from the west, where we are confronted by the Norman west end with its twin towers. The Transitional Period towered facade appears more austere than Southwell due to its plainness. Apart from the C15 replacement of battlemented tops with crocketted corner pinnacles to the twin towers, in place of what must have been original pyramidal roofs, it appears much as completed in late C.12. There are shallow corner buttresses with roll moulding, reaching almost to the tops of the towers. The belfry stage is small with twinned two light windows with small pointed openings under twin arches on shafts. The big central west window is original, round-headed and plain with only the jambs relieved with dogtooth decoration. The only lively ornamentation is to the central doorway, with a lesser extent on the doorway nearby in the north tower. The central doorway has three orders on three shafts with large nailhead decoration between and capitals carved with waterleaf. The arches are ornamented with elaborated forms of chevron, zig-zag and a final ring of dogtooth close to the door - (note also the grotesque masks at the label stops). The door is decorated with fine elaborate scrolled ironwork branching out from the meeting of the doors - modern work imitating the ancient work of the south door.

To fully appreciate the proportions of the church it should be viewed from the south, where the original approach was from the great gatehouse. When built, the church was a remarkable 360ft in length, over twice as long as the surviving nave of 135ft. The side elevations of the nave are simple - plain eaves courses with wavy hebule moulding to the corbel bottom. Clerestory windows are round headed, with large nail head decoration to the hood mould. There are larger imitation Romanesque windows to the aisles inserted in 1845-49 replacing Decorated period ones. Shallow pilaster buttresses are spaced between. On the south side is a typical Nottinghamshire C13 porch with battlemented parapet and an inside stone vault. It is particularly notable for its late C12 door with elaborate iron scrollwork set in a Norman arch of three orders and attached shafts.

Dogtooth decoration, the nave, Worksop.

The interior is a wilful composition quite unlike the earlier Norman work at Blyth and Southwell. The three offer fascinating contrasts across the two century range of the Norman period into the Transitional. The nave was clearly started from the east as was normal. After building the first bay there was a change of ideas. The round piers of the first bay have round capitals with shallow ornamental scallops - of some similarity to Southwell Minster. Bases are plain and square. The arcade arches are decorated with archings and billet ornament. The rest of the nave's nine bays have alternating circular and octagonal pier capitals and are sparely decorated with upstanding stiff formalized leaves in variety, but none in natural form - upper parts are octagonal with spaced bold dogtooth. Below are moulded shallow waterholding bases. The arches are moulded with multi-rolls in complexity, and more dogtooth to the hoodmould. The triforium stands on a string course and is unusual. The arches centred over the arcade below, are separated by arched slots aligned over the piers. The effect of this giving a particular rhythmic movement, heightened by the intrusion of the larger arches into the plain clerestory above. These arches have attached columns supporting single order arches. The heads of the slots have dogtooth decoration to their hoodmoulds. The clerestory windows are unusually placed aligning above the slots and ground floor piers - plain round headed with attached columns and a roll head. There is a further tenth bay between the west towers.

A western gallery was installed in 1760, but was removed in 1845-49 when major renovations included the present timbered roof to the nave. New windows were put into the aisles at this date.

The aisles are original, as is their quadripartite vaulting. The north aisle was built before the south one as can be seen by the differing ribs. In the north aisle are three doorways, a low one from the side entrance, then a large one from the former cloister. A third doorway near the north transept, also off the former cloister was the Canons principal entry into their church. A single plain piscina in the end of the south aisle marks the former chantry of St Leonard, founded in 1300.

The Lady Chapel after surviving roofless for almost 400 years was nearly pulled down in 1847, but was saved on the initiative of the then vicar - Reverend Appleton. After its restoration in 1922 it was dedicated as a memorial chapel to the dead of the 1914-18 war. The chapel is of two bays with triple lancets to each one. Slender side shafts to windows have fillets, with composite shafts between the lancets, all with bell caps. In the corners of the room are corbels with the beginnings of springings for a stone vault, clearly abandoned at an early date in the building but for an unknown reason. The infill wall on the north side, and the screen within the original area on the west date from 1922. The roof is now dark wood, with moulded beams and flat panels. In the south wall is a double piscina set in an arch with two orders over short shafts. Adjacent is a single sedilia similarly treated.

Disappointingly no ancient furnishings survive in the church, and few memorials of note. In the north wall of the north transept is what appears to be a gabled six seater sedilia in rich Decorated period style, the overpainting now rather faded. This was designed by Sir George Gilbert Scott in about 1850 and given by the Duke of Newcastle

EAST LEAKE St Mary

The old village in a dip in the Wolds is now much enlarged by C20 housing, initially encouraged by the opening in 1899 of the Great Central Railway, with the local station providing a new fast link from Nottingham. The ancient church stands prominent in the heart of the

as a reredos when the wall across the nave was the east end. The reredos was resited here when the present north transept was built in 1932. The square Victorian font of 1857 with carved foliage, set on short columns and sited at the end of the north aisle, replaced the Norman one. In 1974 a pleasing new tapering tub font was installed in a more central position in the nave central aisle. There is a Jacobean communion table surviving in the church.

At the central crossing above the high altar is a fine modern corona crafted in wrought iron, brass and coloured lump glass.

In the north aisle wall is a low arched tomb recess with moulded arch on stub columns - now vacant but obviously of some importance, the occupant's name lost in time. On the south aisle wall an engraved brass panel set in a worn alabaster surround commemorates Dame Mary Lassells d.1615. Another, later brass set in the floor by the new font bears a warning verse "Thus falls ye cedar . . ." In the end of the south transept are the mutilated remains of three important alabaster tomb chest effigies, clearly not in their original positions. The two men are in armour, but with their legs cut off below the knee - Lord Thomas Furnival (The Hasty) Treasurer of England (d.1366), his sister Lady Joan Neville (d.1395) in gown and head-dress of the time, and her husband Sir Thomas Neville, Treasurer of England (d.1406), with couchant lion.

There is no ancient glass. The good Victorian glass in the aisle windows unfortunately was reset as panels in clear glazing in 1968. The coloured glass dates mainly from the 1860s and may be by David O'Connor.

East Leake Church from the south-west.

village, close by the Sheepwash Brook running down the main street, with its churchyard raised above the road level by centuries of burials.

The nave and tower are both of Norman period, possibly late C11. The tower is plain and substantial. The battlements are a later addition of the C15, as is the plain needle spire. Inside, high-up on the end wall to the nave is an original round arched opening.

The north wall of the nave is of coarse rubble stone with a substantial extent of herringbone pattern work in typical Norman fashion. In this wall are two early small windows and traces of a north doorway. On the south side there is a narrow aisle added in the early C14, and separated from the nave by an arcade of octagonal piers with plain caps apart from one with crude nailhead decoration. Above are pointed arches. Note the two heads projecting between the springings of the arches, one a cleric who has been watching here for some six hundred years. The south aisle roof beams bear a date of 1638 and the delightful inscription that - "Richard Hutchinson and his sons did frame this work that here is mayde. And at it they all wrought full sore that when they had done they might be payde."

The nave roof was raised in the C15 and the clerestory has two-light flat headed windows. The low pitched roof is of the same date, the timbers bear the inscription IT 1769 but this is probably a repair date. Note also the carved foliated bosses. The chancel dates from the early C14 but was rebuilt reusing much of the original material. The group of three Early English lancet windows within one arch, although restored, are largely original. The finest feature here is the early C14 east window of 5 lights with curvilinear ogee tracery and pointed quatrefoils, all now filled with Victorian stained glass by Kempe, in memory of a Rector who served here for 46 years.

Vamping horn, East Leake.

The font in the end of the south aisle is C13, a very plain octagon on a later pedestal and legs. Adjacent in the rear of the church are several crudely cut bench pews of around 1500; others date from 1612 and 1632.

Outside on the buttresses of the south aisle are the worn remains of two mass clocks, ancient sundials. Holes mark where a stick would be pushed in to cast the shadow to read on the inscribed marks. There is also a much more recent slate sundial west of the porch.
In the churchyard are numbers of the elegantly inscribed C18 headstones of Swithland slate, typical of many South Nottinghamshire churchyards along the Vale of Belvoir. An attractive one of 1805 stands up against the south end of the south aisle and commemorates a William Marcer and his wife. Just east of the

chancel east wall is a fine table tomb of a John Bley, also commemorated by a stained window in the chancel, a local benefactor who endowed a school here in the C18.

But against all these delights, the church is usually more well known for an oddity that it houses, a great long metal trumpet now fixed to the aisle wall. This curious instrument commonly known as a vamping horn, is in reality a form of megaphone invented in 1670 for shouting orders to people at a distance. It was also used in a number of churches by principal singers of the choir to project their voices. Last used in 1855 it is a rarity since only eight other examples survive in the country.

BUNNY St Mary

A small village with an unusual name, unconnected with rabbits. It is more especially known for its eccentric but remarkable Baronet, the wrestling Sir Thomas Parkyns. St Mary's is perhaps the largest church in South Nottinghamshire and with particularly interesting features. A church is recorded in Domesday but nothing survives above ground before building of the late 1200s.

The nave and aisles, all in small random rubble stonework, is Early English and dates from the 1200s, with a building period over into the early 1300s. This can be seen from the differences in the detail and heights of the north and south arcades to the aisles; the south aisle being slightly earlier. The arcades were further modified with octagonal piers on the bay next to the west tower when this was added. Notice the elementary carving of sinuous tendrils and stiff buds on the pier cap on the end pier to the south arcade. The tower is late Decorated period towards the mid-1300s. It is plain and lofty, all in ashlar, with stepped angle buttresses, connected at the top with a broad band just below the battlemented top, crowned with small pinnacles at the corners. Rising above is a

Bunny Church from the south-east.

needle spire with small, sparingly spaced crockets running up the angles, an unusual decoration on Nottinghamshire spires. There is a tall west window, and a high belfry arch inside. Single louvered windows on each face to the belfry, in which hangs a peal of six bells dating from 1590 to 1740.

The delightful south porch was added later in 1425. Like several other Nottinghamshire churches it has a stone roof on stone ribs like a tilt frame of a wagon. There are two little unglazed traceried windows, a niche above the entrance for a figure of the dedication, and inside are stone benches along each side. Porches were important for conducting village business in mediaeval times and most have these seats. The eaves course below the battlements is enriched with a running panel of recessed quatrefoils and there were pinnacles at the corners. The parapet of the south aisle was altered to match at the same time. Looking further it can be seen that all along the nave clerestory and chancel parapets are the remains of pinnacles, which when complete must have given a very rich effect to the church. The clerestory windows are a later insertion, late 1400s, with the differing quatrefoil band here probably of the same date.

The chancel is unusually large, almost equalling the nave in length. In 1346 the church was given to the Austin Canons of Ulverscroft Priory in Charnwood and the lower parts of the chancel were built. The Black Death stopped work in 1348. It was not until 1354 that work was re-started following pressure from the Archbishop and promise of the majority of the income of the church. The windows have intersecting tracery and are from the earlier date, although

Bunny Church, interior looking east.

recast in the C18. The large east window was altered to a square headed, almost domestic form in 1725. There are two small flat headed late 1400s windows above the vestry. This room is thought to have been a small chapel originally, since it has a plain piscina and aumbry in its south wall. Inside, the chancel is all brightness through the large extent of C18 clear glass and the white plastered walls. The chancel roof was altered in 1725; the nave also, possibly a little earlier in 1718. Both roofs are curious in having several bays almost flat supported on massive plain tie beams, but with the remaining bays a little more pitched on shallow trusses. All roof timbers are very plain apart from a section of moulded ridge beam in the nave. In the south wall of the chancel is a pretty traceried double piscina alongside a handsome stepped three seater sedilia with moulded ogee arches topped with rather thick foliated finials. In the north wall is an aumbry with the moulded frame only surviving to the lower parts. These all just pre-date the building halt of the Black Death. The south aisle was originally a side chapel - a small plain piscina survives. In the north aisle wall by the north door is a squint. It had been blocked up, but has been re-opened. Not quite as it was, since it now views the second window in the south aisle, rather than properly viewing the site of the altar to the former chapel.

There is little of older furnishings. Old pews, including the Hall pew with its comfort of fireplace and chimney were taken out in around 1887. The gentry used to enter the church by a small door below the western window in the chancel. This and the window above have now been blocked with stone, probably when the organ was installed. Across the chancel arch is the mutilated remains of a C15 screen, cut down from its original width and repositioned, so that it is now asymmetrical and with a modern top fitted. Surprisingly there are two fonts - a C19 octagonal one at the end of the south aisle, and an ancient tub font at the end of the north aisle reinstalled in 1912. This old one was found early this century on Bunny moor; it is probably C11 and originally from the church. High above the chancel arch are three hatchments, and a painted Royal Arms of George III stands above the south door.

Sir Thos. Parkyns monument, Bunny.

There are a number of interesting monuments. A low arch over an alcove in the wall of the south aisle would have been for a monument. Set in the floor here is the remains of an inscribed C14 grave slab. In the south aisle is the oldest of the wall monuments, a small rather worn one to Humphrey Barlowe (d.1571) and now missing its inscription. The Barlowes had inherited the Manor of Bunny through marriage from the C15 Illingworths. Humphrey's widow married Richard Parkyns bringing the Parkyns family to Bunny. Richard Parkyns's (d.1603) and his wife Elizabeth's (d.1608) monument is in the chancel. They kneel facing each other in prayer, a typical pose of the time, flanked by their four sons and four daughters, an ambitious composition. The most famous but unusual monument is to Sir Thomas Parkyns - moved from the chancel to the north aisle in 1912. It was executed in his own lifetime and depicts him standing ready to wrestle in the Cornish manner. In the adjacent panel is an inscription and below, a small figure laid low by that of Time alongside. Sir Thomas (1633-1741) was a scholar at Westminster School and Cambridge University. An extraordinary man of great energy and an eccentric. He involved himself in architecture, designing farmhouses and other buildings in Bunny and Bradmore on his estate, a school in Bunny, and the strange theatrically ornamented tower and belvedere built on to the old Hall. He was a trained lawyer and sat as a Justice of the Peace in Nottinghamshire and adjacent Leicestershire. He was interested in mathematics, Greek and Latin, compiling a grammar in the latter. He was a bell ringer and an athlete. His great joy was wrestling and he kept himself in training by maintaining two wrestlers in his service. He became known as the Wrestling Baronet, wrote a book entitled the Cornish-Hugg Wrestler and started an annual wrestling match in Bunny. A great eccentric, but a generous benefactor of the two villages.

In the chancel are several other good wall monuments - one to Anne Parkyns (d.1725) the mother of Sir Thomas, by Edward Poynton of Nottingham is particularly interesting - the hour glasses are unusual. A heavy design by a London firm for Thomas Boothby Parkyns, 1st Baron Rancliffe (d.1800). A beautiful carved memorial depicting a girl mourning over a sarcophagus, to Sir Thomas Parkyns (d. 1806) by John Bacon a major London sculptor. There are several other Parkyns memorials in the chancel and grave slabs in the paving. In the south aisle are three simple tablets to members of the Cropper family, from 1787 to 1800. All have similarities, in a delicate Adam style, with a common theme of a funerary urn above. The earliest may be by James Wallis of Newark, the last is by Peck of Loughborough.

Outside in the churchyard are numerous Swithland slate headstones in the South Nottinghamshire tradition; unfortunately all are laid flat and almost overgrown with grass.

EDWINSTOWE St Mary

Edwinstowe has its origins in a forest clearing from which an important settlement grew. Legend says that its name derives from the Christian King Edwin of Northumbria who was killed in a battle in 633, which is reputed to have

Edwinstowe Church from the east.

been nearby. Tradition has another story, that Robin Hood wed the Fair Maid Marion in Edwinstowe Church. The village and its surrounds have changed over the centuries, perhaps the most significant impact being the sinking of the nearby Thoresby coal mine in 1925 which led to extensive new housing. Nevertheless, there are still forest glades immediately north and the heart of the old village still maintains much of its earlier character. The church with sturdy spire is a dominant element, a most pleasing composition set in a large green churchyard, the older part dotted with C18 headstones of local stone, glowing with the russet tints and bright orange splashes of lichen growth.

At first glance the church ensemble could be taken to be of the Perpendicular or late mediaeval period, but a closer look reveals it to be much earlier. The tower is of substantial proportions and has 3 foot thick walls. It was begun in around 1175. There are three stages and on each face of the upper one there is a Norman three arched blank window. On the west wall there is an extraordinarily tall narrow lancet window of the C13, particularly unusual by having a dividing transom. The tower is topped by a broad broach spire. Eight delicate pinnacles with free standing corner columns added in the 1600s enhance the composition. Four of these stand on the corner broaches, and a matching four frame openings in the spire faces. The spire has been damaged three times by lightning - after damage in 1665 it was largely rebuilt in 1680. There is a great arch inside the lower part of the tower. Look for the startling heads under the springings of the arch - one with staring eyes and the other with tongue in open mouth - were these the masons caricaturing each other?

Interior looking west, Edwinstowe.

There was a Saxon church here but nothing survives. The Early English north aisle with an arcade of round columns, caps and bases was added in the 1200s but the windows are mainly C15 replacements. The south aisle with Decorated period arcade of octagonal columns and caps was added in about 1340 to form a chantry chapel to Our Lady and St Margaret of Antioch. The altar stone was removed in Henry VIII's reign but was reinstated when the south aisle was re-dedicated as a War Memorial Chapel after the First World War. The simple south side windows are curiously earlier and, of typical late C13 form. A similar window survives in the north aisle. It is possible that the two aisles are of comparable early date but that the south arcade was not inserted and finished until later. Notice the variety of heads of Kings, clerics and people at the springings of the arcade arches on all sides. One head is reputed to be that of Henry II and opposite, Thomas à Becket whom he caused to be killed in 1170. The rebuilding of the church in 1175 is supposed to be one of the acts of atonement by the King.

The south porch is in ashlar, like the nave clerestory and the parapets, all probably of the same date - late 1300s. The chancel had some rebuilding in about 1600, but the original Norman period priest's door survives.

Furnishings in the church are all fairly modern, with Victorian pews added in 1848. A wooden lectern of about the same time was carved by W. A. Tudsbury, a local crafsman, and was exhibited at the Great Exhibition of 1851. The chancel altar table was also made locally as a memorial to a father and son killed in the First World War. An earlier Jacobean altar table survives as a book stall. There is a plain mediaeval aumbry in the chancel and a piscina in the south aisle. The C14 font is a simple octagon relieved with a middle band of quatrefoils on each face. The elaborately carved chancel screen follows an earlier tradition but is as recent as 1939.

The glass is all Victorian apart from a tiny fragment of mediaeval glass surviving in a window in the north aisle. The chancel east window was a gift in 1861, but perhaps the more interesting artistically is the Foljambe Memorial window of 1873 by Heaton Butler and Bayne. An oddity is the miniature Rigley-Ward family Mausoleum built out from the north aisle in the early C19. Adjacent is a mutilated Christ on the Cross from a wayside calvary in France, brought after the 1914-18 War. Also in this wall is a projecting stone known as the Forest Measure thought to be an ancient standard for measurement. There are no other memorials of especial note.

There are literary connections with Dr Cobham Brewer who died at the Vicarage in 1897, remembered for his 'Dictionary of Phrase and Fable.' Also the Rev F. C. Day-Lewis, Vicar from 1918-38 was the father of Cecil Day-Lewis poet, created Poet Laureate in 1968 and writer of detective novels under the pseudonym Nicholas Blake. This latter making another sort of connection with a gravestone in the churchyard commemorating a Bow Street Runner, forerunner of our police.

HAWTON All Saints

This delightful building contains within its chancel some of the most remarkable stone carving within a small parish church.

Hawton Church from the south-west.

Domesday Book records that there were two churches at Hawton but there are no remains of these. The village is now only a hamlet and nothing of the ancient hall of the Compton and Molyneux families survives.

The earliest parts of the church are the north aisle, its arcade built in around 1280 is of three bays with octagonal piers and matching moulded caps supporting double chamfered pointed arches. The hoodmould above is lined with dogtooth ornament. The arcade is noteworthy for its contrasting responds - a demi-column with ring shaft at the east end and a bracket in the form of a man's head at the west. The south aisle and arcade are similar but later, built in the early 1300s, about the same time as the chancel.

Detail of sedilia, Hawton. The pelican in piety.

The chancel is the great glory of the church, built by Sir Robert de Compton who died in 1330. Of Ancaster ashlar the three bays have bold gabled buttresses between the three light windows, with geometrical cusped roundels in the tops.
The middle window on the south side is curiously and rather wilfully cut away at the foot to accommodate the priest's door. Around the base of the walls is a richly moulded plinth.

Base of Easter Sepulchre, Hawton.

The great seven light east window almost fills its wall. In complete contrast to the side windows its tracery is a wonder of elaborate and exciting cusped ogee curves forming an infinite variety of shapes, or mouchettes.

But even this exceptional window is eclipsed by the wonderful stone carving of the matchless Easter Sepulchre, the sedilia, and piscina. The Easter Sepulchre is part of an overall composition which has the Founder's Tomb placed centrally. A stone effigy of Sir Robert lies there but badly defaced. Above is an ogee arch boldly cusped, and sub-cusped with figures. Rich knobbly foliated crockets decorate the upper curve, rising to a finial with the figure of a bishop on top. To the left, separated by tall pinnacles is a doorway with several orders, half-shafts and another ogee arch - the crowning finial supporting another, smaller bishop figure. The doorway is blocked but formerly gave entrance to a small chapel or chantry - now gone. It is said that this could have been the hermitage of a Peter de Whitelegge who was at the Chapel of St Wilfred at Hawton in 1330. A squint survives in the recess above the effigy, which would have given a view of the high altar to someone on their knees in prayer in the chantry.

To the right is the Easter Sepulchre proper, an exceptional piece, richly carved and probably by the same masons who created the superb pulpitum at Southwell Minster. Above the base the upper part is divided into three, by tall slender pinnacles. The base is in four panels, each with a moulded frame, with sitting sleeping soldiers depicted below an ogee arch in each panel. On the back wall of the recessed main section is the figure of Christ, flanked by angels, portrayed as rising again, with the three Marys in wonder to the right. On the left is a niche to contain the consecrated host until Easter morning when it would be taken to the High Altar as symbolic of the Resurrection. Above the recess are ogee arches, the central one surmounted by a finialled gable. Lean-to decorations like flying buttresses appear in the outer bays. All this work is decorated with a profusion of foliage, with undercut leafwork on the capitals of the attached shafts. In the bands above, relief figures of the Apostles gaze upward at the vision of the Ascension - the feet of Christ seen just disappearing upward into the cornice decoration, flanked by angels heads and with even his footprints visible on the finial below.

The triple sedilia on the opposite wall is almost equally wonderful. There are dividing moulded columns with half caps and cusped ogee arches, the cusps enriched with carved foliage bosses - each arch emphasised with richly leafed crocketted gables.

Carved oak decoration on west door, Hawton.

Within these gables are two bishops and a king, St Edmund, standing on branching foliage. In the spandrels are carved six saints being crowned by angels in the cornice. At the springings are beautifully carved groups - a pelican in piety feeding her young - two men cutting grapes - and crouching creatures at the ends. The whole is a riot of wonderful carving, amazingly crisp after 600 and more years. To the left is a superb double piscina, ogee arched above several miniature orders, with demi-columns and capitals. The great upward flow of the overall ogee arch is decorated with climbing foliage and the top crowned with a great foliated finial. At the springings there is a harpist on one side, and a figure with another stringed instrument on the other side. Words are inadequate to convey the superlative creative craftsmanship and it has to be seen.

The west tower is a fine ambitious creation - late Perpendicular work of about 1480, built at the behest of a later Lord of the Manor, Sir Thomas Molyneux. Built in thin blue lias stones it has ashlar wrap-around buttresses in fine Ancaster limestone. The faces are relieved with moulded string course bands and an accentuated plinth. The belfry stage has paired windows delightfully gathered together under an ogee hoodmould rising to the parapet. The top is capped with a frieze carved in diamonds with infill quatrefoils and shields with grotesque gargoyles at the corners.

The battlements are refined with moulded gabled merlons, between panelled ones which rise to eight crocketted finials. The typical large west window with panel tracery stands above the ornamented west doorway with shields bearing the Molyneaux arms, a punning heraldic 'cross moline' in the spandrels. The door is original, with sinuous tracery which incorporates elaborated M's. Across the centre rail are the remains of the inscription 'Jesu Mercy Lady Helpe.' There are four bells in the tower. Two cast and marked from George Oldfield's foundry in Nottingham in 1655. Another is dated 1624. The fourth is undated but older.

The nave clerestory was added contemporary with the tower in 1480 and the two aisles were modified on their north, south and west faces with inserted three-light round headed windows and four centre arches, except the western ones which are straight pointed. The moulded battlements to the nave and aisles were added at the same time.

The east end windows in the two aisles are earlier insertions contemporary with the building of the chancel after 1330, the three light north-east one having writhing tracery in company with the great east window.

Inside, there are large elaborate canopied niches for saints in the end of each aisle. One incorporating the intriguing initials AR. There are small plain piscinas in the side walls from when these were side chapels. In the south wall is an unoccupied low recess - originally for an effigy.

Across the chancel is a C15 oak screen, with six bays on either side the entrance arch of three bays. There is carved tracery in the upper part of each bay, with solid panels in the dado pierced only with single quatrefoils. A rare sight is in the arcade wall above, where the roughly sawn off end of the original rood loft can be seen.

The plain mid C14 octagonal font is surprisingly small. The nave and aisles are filled with plain substantial pews in thick oak, C15 with very little restoration. Apart from a few fragments of grisaille there are no stained windows. There are few monuments. Under the tower in the floor is the matrix stone, with brasses missing, to Sir Robert de Compton d.1308 father of the builder of the chancel. Another matrix stone to an unknown lies in front of the north door. There is a wall monument of a truncated obelisk with cartouche and urns all in marble, to Alexander and Mary Holden (d.1769) who bought an estate at Hawton. There are later unassuming wall plaques which are of interest because of the connections with the Holdens of that other architectural treasure the lost house Nuthall Temple, disgracefully demolished in 1929.

NEWARK *St Mary Magdalene*

A great parish church and one of the finest town churches in the country - over 220 feet long with a 250 feet high steeple. This splendid tower with lofty spire soars above the town and is a landmark for miles over the Trent Valley. The town is still predominantly Georgian in character with a mediaeval street pattern surrounding the market place. The church close by is almost entirely concealed by buildings around. This masks the scale of the church, except from the north and when inside. There was a Saxon settlement at Newark but no trace remains of that church. Around 1100 the manor

Newark Church from the south-east.

and church were granted to the Bishop of Lincoln and the building of a new Norman church began. The present crypt dates from that time, and incorporated into the nave crossing piers are pillars from that period. The position of these pillars indicates that like the present church the Norman one was also cruciform in shape.

The angle buttressed tower was begun in about 1220 in the Early English style. The detail is elaborately ornate. The west doorway has an acute arch and deeply recessed orders ornamented with dog tooth pattern, arising from attached shafts. Inset is a fine old oak door. Adjacent is blank arcading in irregular form, with above, the surprising insertion of a large and much later Perpendicular period window. The second stage above is later C13 with a pair of windows, continued beyond in matching blank arcading, with the wall surface above the arches carved with bold trellis pattern - similar and contemporary with Lincoln Cathedral. The belfry stage is of the Decorated period with twinned windows in each face surmounted with an unusual crocketted gable form. In the gables and low between the buttresses and the windows are niches with surviving statues of the apostles. The top of the tower has a recessed quatrefoil frieze supported on a row of carved heads and with crocketted corner pinnacles. The setback needle spire has four tiers of lucarnes arranged on alternating faces and richly decorated with crocketted gables.

The body of the church has an almost wholly Perpendicular character, but a closer look shows the south aisle to be of the earlier Decorated period with flowing ogee tracery in the windows. This aisle appears to have been the first stage in a planned rebuild of the church, but must have been arrested by the problems of the mid to late 1300's, Rebuilding didn't recommence until some 50 years later when the nave and chancel were gradually taken down and rebuilt in the new Perpendicular style. The last parts to be added were the transepts completed in 1539. The view from the north presents a wonderful wall of glass with the large four light nave and chancel windows, and an almost continuous line of glazing in the clerestory windows. As the work progressed the ratio of glass to stone wall increased dramatically bringing about the wonderful soaring lines of the great east window to the chancel, and the almost all "glass and ribs" ends to the transepts.

The earlier south aisle has richly treated buttresses with niches for now lost statues, projecting carved figures, and crocketted gabled heads. All along the string course below the embattled parapet are carved figures. The battlemented parapets of the chancel and its aisles are enriched with rows of recessed quatrefoil panels and shields. The aisle end parapets are further enlivened with grotesque faces. The chancel aisles are elaborated with tall detached and linked pairs of pinnacles rising out of each buttress. The end of the chancel has a pair of buttresses which are inexplicably similar to the earlier Decorated period ones of the nave south aisle. These again have projecting figures in lively activity - two men in a boat being pushed off by another man, two men quarrelling and pulling each other's hair. Above in a niche over the east window is the figure of the patron saint, Mary Magdalene. There is a fine Perpendicular period porch on the south side fronting the earlier nave aisle; note how one of the windows is cut into. The upper room of the porch contains a library established in 1698 by Bishop White, a former Vicar of Newark. Inside, there is a great feeling of space and wonderful lightness. Tall slender piers of the nave have attached shafts with small foliated caps and included faces. There is a great upward feeling towards the clerestory and roof, but simultaneously the eye is drawn onward to the screen, the chancel, and the great east window. The ceilings are almost flat, the nave and chancel ones richly decorated in colour to the ribs, bosses and panels. Along the perimeter are flying angels echoing the rows of carved angels at the arch springings below. Before the chancel arch is a magnificent carved oak screen made in 1508, the only surviving work from the famed workshop of Thomas Drawswerd of York. Highly intricate with tracery work and elaborate canopy, the screen carries round backing the choir stalls along the chancel arcades. The choir stalls are of the same date. Beneath the seats of the rear stalls are an outstanding set of twenty six carved misericords. Between the sanctuary and chancel aisles, there are, on opposites sides, two chantries in stone, not exceptional in design but in excellent condition. The earlier one on the north side was built for Thomas Meyring in 1500, paid for out of wool sales and endowed with a flock of sheep. The other, founded by

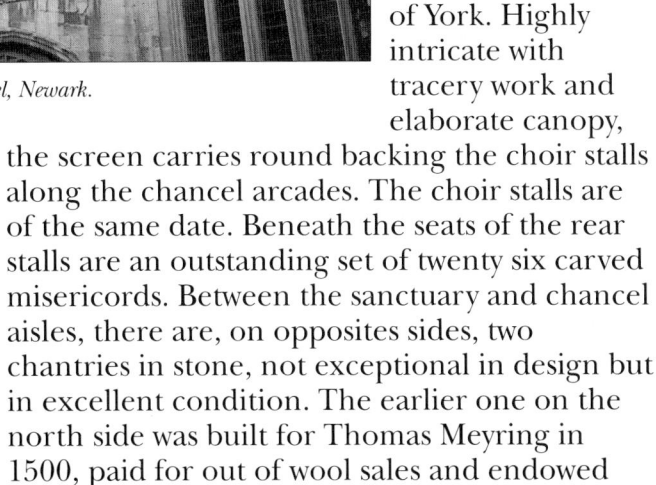

South transept and south side of chancel, Newark.

48

Robert Markham in 1506, is very similar in form but a little more refined. Between two of the mullions are two inset C16 painted panels, in naive style, illustrating the mediaeval concept - the "Dance of Death" - reputedly one of only two surviving examples in England. One figure, a lordly young man, purse in hand, the other his dancing skeleton holding a rose. The chancel side aisles have low wrought iron screens and gates from 1887. Between the windows along the outer walls of these aisles are tall niches for missing statues, with crocketted canopies, and carved brackets below of heads or reclining figures.

East of the raised sanctuary is an ambulatory with three chapels in parallel. The central one is the Lady Chapel; its great window glowing with Victorian glass in memory of the late Prince Consort Albert, of 1862, an important example of John Hardman and Co's work. The south side chapel is dedicated to the Holy Spirit. Its magnificent six light window filled with fragments of mediaeval glass renovated and arranged by Miss Joan Howson in 1957. The centre two lights have C14 glass, earlier than the building, and includes Adam and Eve being sent out from Eden. The glass in the outer four lights is mainly C15 and paler in colour, containing scenes from the Passion and Resurrection of Christ. The northward chapel is to St George, the woodwork designed by W. D. Caröe, and used as the Sherwood Foresters' regimental chapel.

The great reredos is an imitation of late C14 work, painted panels with scenes, saints and Christ's life, almost overpowering from the brilliance of its gilding. Dating from as recent as 1937 it is by (Sir) Ninian Comper. Behind is the original stone screen. On the ambulatory side of this is a sedilia of 13 stone seats, each with a carved canopy with leaf finials and enlivened with tiny heads of people and animals. Added above is a large mosaic panel illustrating the Adoration of the Lamb executed by James Powell and Sons of Whitechapel in 1912. Central to this sedilia are stone steps leading down to the two bay crypt, of late C12 date with keeled ribs and two bosses. In 1981 it was converted into a treasury for church plate. The major display is of the Lady Leake Bequest of 1705 which provided replacement for the church plate lost during the Civil War.

There are other noteworthy features, fittings and memorials. On one of the north piers of the crossing is a bracket carved as a falling figure of a king run through with a sword. More bizarre, are two stone bracket faces set in the west wall of the nave north aisle, the upper figure has twin faces, the one below with 3 noses and 4 eyes.

The font is another curiosity. It was damaged by parliamentarian soldiers in the Civil War. The C15 lower part survives, but the upper part is a replacement of 1665. In consequence the lower halves of the saints depicted in the panels have C15 dress, but with the later upper halves oddly Stuart figures with beards and moustaches of that period.

One of the greatest treasures is in the chancel aisle - a great Flemish made brass - approximately 10 feet by 6 feet, commemorating Alan Fleming a rich merchant who died in 1361. In the Lady Chapel is a black Purbeck marble tomb chest of Robert Browne High Sheriff, a C16 benefactor of the town and Constable of the Castle. On the wall of the chancel south aisle is an alabaster memorial to Hercules Clay who died in 1645 and was so disturbed by dreams that his house would be hit during the Civil War siege that he moved out, just before it did happen. In the chancel north aisle on a pillar a memorial to John Johnson, Alderman and Mayor, (died 1659) with his painted bust set in an oval niche under a triangular pediment. There are two rather similar ones within the choir - Robert Ramsey (died 1639) with broken pediment over and scrolls - also Thomas Atkinson (died 1661). In the south transept is a fine wall monument to Daniel Crayle (died 1727), a bust on a pedestal with a pediment above, drapery, and cartouche below. There is also one in rococo style to Anne Taylor (died 1757), by the great sculptor Roubiliac. An elegant wall plaque in the north transept is a 1939-45 War Memorial - by Robert Kiddey in Eric Gill manner stylizing the Descent from the Cross.

There is more good Victorian glass by William Wailes, and C E Kemp in the nave south aisle. One window by Gerente is particularly rich in colour. The tower window glass of 1887 is by Burlison and Grylls.

One other notable monument is to Anne Markham (died 1601). It was formerly in Cotham church but is now on the south aisle wall, near to the font. It is of particularly fine workmanship and depicts her kneeling, with sons and daughters around as weepers. Elegant with a good classical surround of Corinthian columns and pediment.

NOTTINGHAM St Mary the Virgin

This is a glorious building - a splendid town church with a nave and transepts of outstanding quality. It is a stately building set high on a rock eminence, twinned by the castle on another. The church siting is now much masked by the closely surrounding C19 commercial buildings, but in mediaeval times it would have dominated the skyline on the southern approach to Nottingham, and filled the traveller with awe.

The site lies within the original Saxon borough

St. Mary's, Nottingham.

and there was probably a Saxon minster here. There was certainly a church here at the time of the Norman Domesday survey in 1086. Although the Normans established a new borough adjacent to their new castle some distance away, it is believed that the old church remained until destroyed in 1171 when the town was sacked by rebels in revolt against Henry II. A new church was built after this but there are no remains surviving above ground.

Detail of painted reredos, St. Mary, Nottingham.

The main elements of the present church are almost entirely C15. Work on this ambitious new church started sometime in the later 1300s. It is known that it was well underway by 1400 since an indulgence of Pope Boniface IX was granted to all who visited and donated to the "wondrous, manifold and sumptuous work there proceeding." The nave, aisles, transept and chancel were all finished by 1475, but the tower was not finished until late in the century, in the reign of Henry VII. This new church was much larger than the previous one and seems to have been built around the earlier walls. This may be one reason why the south porch is so far eastward, as it is located on the alignment of a predecessor. The porch is early 1400s and has a stone tunnel vaulted roof, not uncommon in Nottinghamshire. The richly sculptured bronze doors inside are by Henry Wilson and date from 1904. The west front of the nave is a fine composition, although it is a reconstruction executed in 1843 of the original west end, working from an engraving of 1677 published in a book by Thoroton, the Nottingham antiquarian. This followed the removal of a classical fronting of 1726 which had replaced the original west front.

C.15 carving in nave, St. Mary, Nottingham

The dominant central tower is of three stages, surmounted by plain battlements crowned with eight elegant pinnacles. The top stage has the unusual feature of an arcade of four windows on each face - the two inner ones pierced and the outer ones blank.

The richness of the composition of the C15 church is enhanced with panelled battlements and frieze below, and arcaded panels on the buttresses. The large chancel is more restrained than the rest of the church, this may have been due to economy on the part of the monks of Lenton Priory who were responsible for this part. The roof dates from Gilbert Scott's restoration work of 1872 and its internal elegant colouring dates from 1965. The south chapel alongside the chancel was added by Temple Moore in 1912, but re-uses the original chancel side windows.

Inside, the wall faces are interestingly arranged in a series of panels divided by plain rolls. The slender nave arcade piers, rather unusually, rise and turn up into arches without any capitals to distinguish the change. The large clerestory windows above are set within the panels, and with those in the aisles, give a particularly even and flowing architectural pattern. The large expanse of windows makes a light interior. The north and south transepts are particular glories. The side walls pierced with this regular pattern of windows, but with the gable ends almost entirely a glazed wall held together with a skeletal arrangements of ribs. The great window areas in the church must have been a wonderful sight when filled with the original mediaeval glass. Only fragments of this now survive in some windows in the south side of the chancel. However, there is a fine display of C19 glass with examples of the work of many distinguished Victorian makers including Clayton and Bell, Burlison and Grylls, C E Kempe and John Hardman.

Nothing much of original church furnishings survives and only partial remains of old monuments. C15 benches and misericord seats were removed to St Stephen's Sneinton in 1848. The font is C15, octagonal with panels. There is a battered alabaster C14 figure in the north aisle. A canopy and effigy of the tomb of John Samon a Mayor of Nottingham who died in 1416 is in the south transept, one of three generations of the family who were benefactors and prime movers behind the rebuilding. In the north transept is a similarly set tomb recess with niches and damaged angel figures - probably the remains of a commemoration to Thomas Thurland (died 1473), Mayor of the town, wool merchant of the Staple and benefactor. Apart from a few other mediaeval fragments the principle monuments are early C19 tablets. An unusual feature is the Royal Arms of about 1710, expressed as individual figures of a Lion and Unicorn, the one bearing the arms of Queen Anne and the other the arms of Nottingham. Of woodwork, the chancel screen and reredos are by Bodley and Garner 1885 and the stalls are by Gilbert Scott in 1872.

In the churchyard are a good group of typical south Nottinghamshire slate headstones, and a very unusual one of 1714 made of pipeclay by William Sefton a well known local pipemaker, in memory of his daughters.

BABWORTH All Saints

The church stands hemmed around with trees on a green bank; a picturesque scene. Now lying at the end of a track, this was the main road from Worksop to Retford until 1816 when the Hon. John Bridgman-Simpson had it diverted away to its present line. This was so as to implement the landscape scheme by Humphrey Repton for the nearby Babworth Hall grounds, which included a lake.

Babworth is unusual in being an extensive parish without a village, only populated with hamlets and scattered houses. Only a few buildings are near the church, the former schoolhouse and two others at the start of the track, and the former rectory rather nearer. This latter is an

Babworth Church from the south-west.

impressive house with extensive stables and outbuildings, it is now renamed Haygarth House and used for offices. It is essentially a C18 house but was substantially extended and elaborated with gables and bays in the early C19. This was by the Rev. W Bridgman-Simpson (Rector 1838-1895) a younger son of the Hon. John Bridgman-Simpson and who was required to provide a house suitable for his bride, the daughter of Earl Fitzwilliam, on their marriage.

The church is essentially all late C15 Perpendicular period, built in ashlar. There is no obvious indication of earlier fabric, although the first building of a church here is recorded in 1290 and attributed to Robert de Swillington a canon of Lincoln.

The chancel and nave are one, with no structural division inside or out. To the north is an aisle as long as the nave section, and divided by an arcade of chamfered arches on octagonal piers with octagonal moulded caps. All is simple and plain except for the mediaeval mason's caprice of carved grotesque faces on the respond brackets. Further along is a small arched opening between nave and aisle, its original purpose lost. Beyond the aisle, filling the north west corner is a C19 vestry in similar style externally. A high arch to the tower reveals an open railed gallery for bellringers. Outside, the regular rhythm of flat headed windows each with three round headed lights, is marked by stepped buttresses. A moulded battlemented parapet has corner and intermediate pinnacles. The church, tower and south porch are bound together with a bold moulded and projecting plinth course. Below the second window from the east is an inserted C16 priest's door. The north aisle is similar except that the easternmost window on the side, surprisingly has four lights to its otherwise matching window. There is a small priest's door also on this north side. The west window of the aisle is all restored stonework with a pointed arch and three lights with panel and reticulated tracery above. Much of the upper part of this gable end is restored work.

The south porch is typically Nottinghamshire pattern with similarities to St Michael's, West Retford. The roof is another stone one supported on four moulded ribs, each terminating in tiny carved features - a man's head, a rosette, a bunch of grapes with leaves, a strange little crouching creature. The parapet is embattled like the nave, but only the gable pinnacle survives. Through the moulded entrance arch are benches down each side.

The tower is low and sturdy with stepped angle buttresses to the western corners. A band runs round below the simple two light belfry windows. Interestingly, these windows and the large west window are all almost round-headed in form. The top of the tower is battlemented with crocketted pinnacles lifting the corners. The church roof is low pitched and slate covered. The timbers were all renewed in 1859-62 during restorations. Further work in 1878 removed inserted galleries including ones for the Bridgeman-Simpson family, and another for the Chapman's of Ranby Hall which is also in the parish. The pulpit dates from 1853, a memorial to a Richard Hodgkinson of Morton Grange. The font is a Bridgeman-Simpson memorial of the mid C19, and the pews are also of that time with comfortably wide seats.

Church clock, Babworth, made by Sharpe of Retford. Inscribed "Watch and pray till he come."

Notice a number still bear the legend FREE on the end.

There are interesting stained windows by important glass artists: the east five light window by William Wailes 1855, the west tower window by C E Kempe 1879. A window in the north aisle has leaded coloured glass designed by the wife of and commemorating the work of the Rector the Reverend Edmund Jessup who retired in 1984. It also celebrates the 700th Anniversary of the church. A rarer treasure is the elegant late Georgian "Resurrection" window of 1830 by Francis Eginton.

Around the walls of the chancel are wall monuments to the Bridgman-Simpson family who came to Babworth through inheritance in the late C17. They are interesting but not outstanding. Worth looking at is the tablet with urn to Rev John Simpson of 1784 signed by Thomas Waterworth, the large William Simpson memorial with relief sarcophagus and obelisk of 1768, the adjacent touchingly small relief casket, to Arthur Bridgman-Simpson midshipman who died at sea of fever in 1827. There are inscribed tablets to the Hon Ann Maria Vane 1759 and Morgan Vane 1789 of the long demolished Bilby Hall, an

54

ancient manor in the extreme west of Babworth parish. Only the base survives of a lost important monument to Henrietta Simpson, herself an artist, and signed by Humphrey Repton the designer and Coade the sculptor.

In the tower hang six bells, three founded in 1691 by Samuel Smith of York, the others as recent as 1959 from the well known foundry of John Taylor and Co of Loughborough.

Among its attractions Babworth is more usually remembered for its connections with the Reverend Richard Clyfton who was rector here from 1586 to 1605. A free-thinker, he preached in his sermons against the rituals of the established church and encouraged others with these ideas. Among those who came to hear him were William Brewster from Scrooby and William Bradford of Austerfield. When Clyfton was deprived of his living for preaching sedition he went to Scrooby, setting up a Separatist church there in 1606 with Brewster. But this affront to church and state was short lived and to escape persecution the little group had to flee to the Netherlands to be able to pursue religious freedom. Clyfton and his wife went with them to Amsterdam. Sadly the Reverend Clyfton, the most senior in age of three founders of the movement, died in 1616 and was denied his rightful place on the historic voyage of the Pilgrim Fathers to America in 1620.

SCROOBY *St Wilfrid*

The village's principal claim to fame is its link with the Pilgrim Fathers through William Brewster and his short establishment of a Separatist Movement church at the Manor House. Apart from this, Scrooby was always of importance through its location on the Great North Road and in having a Manor House of the Archbishops of York.

Scrooby Church from the south-east.

The church is a pleasing composition and is dedicated to St Wilfrid, a Bishop of York who died in 709. The earliest known references to the church are in the late C12 when it was a Chapel of Ease of Sutton-cum-Lound, and when it was appropriated to the Chapel of St Mary and Holy Angels at York. Low Street by the east side of the churchyard was originally the route of the Great North Road through the village. A grey stone wall retains the raised burial ground along this road and adjacent Church Street, terminating in the former pinfold. Adjacent to this is the timber framed house, a former vicarage or curate's house of circa 1590. The churchyard extension runs to the rear of this and up to the Turnpike diversion of the Great North Road of 1766. The overall appearance of the church is of the Perpendicular Period. The tower dates from the early 1400s, the rest of the building is about 1500. The tower is short with a plain spire. It is unusual in having an inward splay of the upper corners of the tower, gathering into an octagonal top. From each splay rise pinnacles topped with crocketted finials. The tops of the pinnacles look cut off and it is possible they were reduced to their present appearance during repairs after serious lightning damage to the steeple in 1817 and 1831. St Michael's at West Retford has similar splays but with little flying buttresses across to the spire. St Wilfrid's could have been similar. There is a fine large west window in the tower and simple 2 light belfry openings. There are particularly large ashlars at the base of the tower and a bold unifying plinth course runs right round the tower and church.

The nave and chancel have a full length south aisle with the slated roof running down as a catslide over the aisle. Although the whole appearance is Perpendicular there is indication that the nave and chancel fabric is older but was given a face-lift in the late C15 when the aisle was built. Mediaeval builders were very adept at inserting new windows, adding parapets, inserting plinths and other new fashionable features.

The moulded battlemented parapet runs all round. It was formerly enriched with pinnacles, but only the bases survive. The windows are Early Tudor with flat heads and simple round headed lights. Stepped buttresses punctuate the walls, with angled ones at the corners. As part of the decorative effect the string course becomes a hood mould over the windows and drops down each side. The large east window of the chancel although of Perpendicular period character, is an insertion of 1864 when the church underwent Victorian "restoration." Its stained glass is later, 1889 by Powells of Leeds. The south porch is late C15, contemporary with the aisle, and has a Nottinghamshire stone roof on internal moulded ribs. The porch now has a squat appearance and heavy plain parapets. It originally must have been more decorated on the top with battlements and pinnacles like the rest of the church. Inside the porch are the usual bench seats. Just inside the church door is a small stone to Penelope Sandys, grand-daughter of the Archbishop Sandys (died 1588), whose tomb is in Southwell Minster. She may well have died while staying at the Archbishop's Manor House. The church interior is simple with an almost wholly Victorian feel. The arcade is of mediaeval octagonal piers but virtually all interior fittings are Victorian. The font and stone pulpit date from 1864 but their bases could be earlier. Pews are C19 except for two curious little free standing benches in the aisle. These have mediaeval panelled bench ends but richly carved backs with bands of vines and bunches of grapes. They are clearly an amalgam of old pieces. Along the south aisle is a small priest's door.

The east end of the aisle is raised up two steps and although it now accommodates the small C19 organ it must originally have been a side chapel or chantry. At the top of the steps is a single pew referred to as Brewster's pew. Although the name is likely to be apocryphal, the pew material is certainly C15, with bench ends and a carved back panel similar to that in the small pews in the aisle. It has been suggested that the vine panels are from a mediaeval chancel screen, but this is questionable.

The quietness of Scrooby today belies its former importance. The first mention of the Archbishop's Manor House was in 1207. In 1212 King John stayed there. Margaret, elder daughter of Henry VII stayed overnight on her way north to marry James IV of Scotland, and would have seen the church as newly built. Cardinal Wolsey, after his fall from power, spent the whole of September 1530 at the Manor. In 1536 the earls of Shrewsbury, Rutland and Huntingdon met there as representatives of Henry VIII in consequence of the rebellion in the north called the Pilgrimage of Grace, following the Dissolution of the Monasteries. Henry VIII himself stayed at Scrooby in 1541 with his Privy Council. Successive Archbishops of York stayed here when visiting the southern parts of their territory.

In 1575 William Brewster senior was appointed Receiver and Bailiff of the Archbishop's estate at Scrooby. Later, in 1588 he was additionally appointed 'Master of the Queen's Poster's responsible for providing lodging and stabling for royal messengers en route along the Great North Road. His son William seems to have been born in about 1566, but date and actual place are uncertain. Since his father was certainly at Scrooby from 1575 the young William must have attended St Wilfrid's Church until he went away to Peterhouse College, Cambridge in 1580; afterwards serving with the English Ambassador in the Netherlands until he returned to Scrooby. Following his father's death he in turn took up the 'Master of Postes' appointment at the Manor House.

Brewster became a free thinker following his Cambridge and Dutch experiences and turned against the formal Anglican Church. In 1598 he was fined in the ecclesiastical courts for irregular attendance at the parish church. He took to visiting places where others had started to preach against the fundamental principles of the established church, such as the hierarchy of bishops and the wearing of clerical vestments. Among these preachers were Richard Clyfton at Babworth and Rev John Smyth at Gainsborough. In 1602 Smyth established a Separatist church in the Old Hall at Gainsborough. In 1605 Clyfton was forced to resign from Babworth and took refuge with Brewster at Scrooby. Brewster established the Scrooby Separatist Church in the Manor House in 1606 with himself as ruling elder, Richard Clyfton as pastor and John Robinson as teacher. This defiance of religious laws could only be short lived and in September 1607 Brewster resigned from his service of 'Bailiff' and 'Master of Postes.' Shortly after, the Scrooby group broke up and following considerable persecution eventually joined Smyth and others in the Netherlands in 1608. Brewster and his family were eventually to be four among the forty original pilgrims on the historic 'Mayflower' voyage to New England in 1620.

TEVERSAL St Catherine

The setting is a delight, a secluded green place of trees and a few stone buildings. It looks northward to the great park of Hardwick Hall and yet is all close to the industrial and urban spread along the old Nottinghamshire and Derbyshire coalfield.

The small church stands in its churchyard flanked by the late C17 former Rectory and on the west side by the spacious drive down to the Manor House - an old house remodelled in 1767 and again in 1896.

The church is built of local coal measures stone, golden and brown. The west tower is C15, plain apart from the stepped irregular spaced battlements around the top. Set in the wall of the south aisle is a fragment of a mediaeval coffin stone incised with a cross, and at the south east corner of the chancel is a sundial with an ancient worn face. Close by the south porch are several early headstones - one

Part of Norman doorway, Teversal.

survivor bearing the date 1681.

Inside the porch is one of the most singular Norman doorways. An outer hood mould terminates in figures of a priest and a dragon's head. Inside this is a row of stones decorated with lozenge pattern around the arch. Down the sides they are differently patterned and mismatched. The inner ring is the most unusual with nineteen medallions bearing figurative carvings - fishes, a dove,

Teversal Church from the south-west.

a leaf, a tree with three leaves, a figure in benediction with a book, a serpent, a six leafed rose and others. Whether there is a theme is unclear. It is possible that the doorway was originally at the west end of the church and was moved here when the tower was built. This could account for the displacement and mismatch. The door is mediaeval, hanging on old hinges and with an ancient lock.

The body of the church is C12 Norman. The arcades were later insertions when the north and south aisles were added. The south aisle is the earlier, probably around the turn of 1200 with round arches carried on circular piers and plain caps - one column is the exception, of quatrefoil shape with fillets in the recesses. The north aisle is later, around 1230-40, with pointed arches instead, but again carried on circular piers and caps, the latter having simple nail head decoration. Crude trefoils and scrolls decorate the arch springing above. There also are two staring mask- like heads and another on the chancel arch. The aisles are very narrow, just wide enough for the ritual processions of their time. It is exceptional that such narrow ones still survive. The south aisle was part widened in the C15, probably for a side chapel.

But inside, the greatest delight is in seeing a mediaeval church completely fitted out with C17 furnishings. The body is filled with box pews of the later 1600's. Particular delights are the two small enclosures either side of the chancel, and the unusually long narrow one down the north aisle. Even the Norman tub font has its own enclosure with doors, and seats inside. Adjacent is the family pew, or 'Squire's Pew' of the Molyneux, raised up with a panelled canopy supported on barley sugar twist corner posts, very much like a large four poster bed. It has an unglazed window to the nave, and is provided with hat pegs. It probably dates from around 1675, like the small west gallery and the nave roof. The latter has king post trusses with some Gothic detail - note the carved bosses, one leafed and the other a grotesque face. Notice also the smaller faces carved at the foot of the wall posts.

The chancel is fitted with Jacobean altar rails on turned balusters and gates. The altar table has the typical bulbous legs of the period.

There are several notable monuments. In the south aisle, hemmed in by the high pews are two incised alabaster tomb slabs - Roger Greenhalgh (d.1563) is portrayed in fur-trimmed gown with hands in prayer, his wife (d.1538) is alongside unportrayed but marked with a large cross. Their estate passed by marriage to the Molyneux family of Hawton. There are four Molyneaux monuments in the chancel. Francis Molyneux Bart (d.1674) in alabaster with his bust in an oval recess. The figure head quite overpowered by the excessive swathes of drapery. The second monument alongside is much finer, an excellent work with the busts of John Molyneux (d.1691) and his wife Lucy (d.1688) set in niches, with cartouches, and a broken pediment above. On the south wall another good monument with two free standing busts on short pedestals to Sir Francis Molyneux (d.1741) and Diana (d.1718) daughter of John Howe of Langar. Nearby is a simple elegant white marble plaque by Joseph Kendrick, with the profile of Sir Francis Molyneux (d.1812) the 7th and last baronet who had served Parliament as Gentlemen Usher of The Black Rod for 47 years. The Earls of Carnarvon inherited and enjoyed the estate until the Dowager Countess died in 1929. Around the clerestory walls of the nave are a particularly fine set of six hatchments of the Molyneuxs and one to a Carnarvon. Their dominance of the upper nave is matched by a Georgian Royal Arms above the chancel arch.

OSSINGTON The Holy Rood

This delightful church stands alone now that Ossington Hall has gone; secret in surrounding woodland, away from the village houses. The only distant glimpse of the church is from the lovely wooded road to Moorhouse, where it can be seen standing above the remains of the lake in the surviving parkland.
In 1144 the church of Ossington was given to the Priory of Lenton, but after 1208 it passed to the Knights Hospitallers of St John of Jerusalem who already held the Manor of Ossington. Following the Dissolution of the Monasteries after 1536 the Manor and Rectory was passed to the Duke of Suffolk who in turn transferred it to a Richard Andrewes soon after in 1543. The daughter of this Andrewes married Edmund Cartwright, and so the estate passed into the gifted Cartwright family. Unfortunately the male line ran out in 1749 on the death of George Cartwright. His four daughters sold the estate to William Denison a wealthy wool merchant who had risen in the world after making a sudden fortune in 1755.

The Cartwrights had built a Tudor house at Ossington, but pulled this down and replaced it in 1729 with a large plain brick house in the new Georgian style. This was enlarged further by the Denisons in 1790, by Lindley, a former assistant of the architect John Carr of York. The Hall was occupied by the family until requisitioned for the military during the 1939-45 war. It was not treated kindly. By 1963 Col. Denison felt the house was becoming too large a burden and so had it demolished, leaving the church in its now isolated position.

William Denison died in 1782 and was succeeded by his brother Robert. He only survived until 1785 but in that time he

Ossington Church from the south.

had the old church taken down and commissioned John Carr to build a new one on the site in classical style, all in ashlar.
John Carr (1723-1807) for some fifty years was the principal architect working in Yorkshire and Northern England. He was a stone mason by training, and his father, grandfather and great-grandfather had all been masons near Wakefield where they owned quarries. Although largely self taught Carr became a most competent architect and very successful in the Georgian age. His wife's father was a 'gentleman' and Carr enjoyed the patronage of the gentry. He is best known in Nottinghamshire for his Newark Town Hall and Assembly Rooms.

The body of the church is a simple rectangle of 5 bays with a slated hipped roof. The windows are tall and round headed - originally all glazed with clear glass for lightness, but several were later filled with coloured glass memorials. The entrance is in the centre of the south front, marked with a gabled portico on plain columns. At the west end is a three stage tower, the upper part set back behind groups of three columns at each corner. The entablature above is surmounted with a drum capped with a small dome and a ball finial. In the tower hangs a six bell peal, the earliest bell dated 1632. Originally there was an octagonal mausoleum attached at the east end but this was removed in 1838.

Inside, the east end bay forms the sanctuary and is divided from the nave section by three simple arches on Tuscan columns. The walls are plastered, with a cove and mouldings at the junction with the flat ceiling. There is an oak panelled dado all round and, along the top runs a text carved in relief, executed by Lady Elinor Denison with help from William Mawson the estate joiner. There are plain oak bench pews, and a handsome oak pulpit with decorated panels also carved by Lady Elinor (d.1939).
A good stained glass window in the south wall by G. Cooper Abbs, commemorates her in glowing blues and greens. There are three other late Victorian stained glass windows, one in memory of Viscountess Ossington the wife of Speaker Ossington. The Denison family achieved particular distinction in the C19, John Evelyn served as Speaker of the House of Commons 1857-72, becoming a Viscount on retirement. A younger brother became Bishop of Salisbury, and another served as Governor-General of Australia.

One of the most interesting features of this small church is the collection of monuments.
In niches in the west wall, on either side of the organ, stand elegant figures of William Denison and his brother Robert. William leans on a stump in country gentleman pose, holding a copy of Alexander Pope's (d.1744) - 'The Universal Prayer.' The brother leans on his books, in a more animated pose, seemingly less concerned to be the country gentleman. Both monuments are by the great and fashionable sculptor Joseph Nollekens. These cost substantial sums at the time, we know that Robert set aside £1,000 in his will for a monument. The worldly figures contrast greatly with the pious grouping on the Elizabethan monument in the sanctuary of William Cartwright and his wife Grace. This is an ambitious and costly wall monument arranged on three levels with projecting entablatures supported by two rows of columns. William in a suit of plate armour kneels facing his wife Grace - at the lowest level their 12 children stand gathered in two groups, all holding prayer books except two, who hold skulls denoting they died in

infancy. Another wall monument in marble is to George Cartwright and his wife Catherine (c.1743), an unusual composition with a centre cartouche flanked by two tall thin obelisks with two flame topped urns. Of competing interest is the tomb chest adjacent, on which are two fine monumental brasses to Reynald Peckham (d.1551) and his wife Elizabeth. She was the daughter of Edmund, the first Cartwright at Ossington. These brasses are particularly important since they are all palimpsests. The effigies have been cut from a German or Flemish brass made originally for a lady in about 1360. The inscription brass at the foot is from one to a lady, engraved in about 1440. The earlier engravings are on the reverse sides so are now concealed. The shields and marginal inscription have also been reused and date from about 1500. It is thought that most of the reused brasses came from some monastic church following the Dissolution.

In front of the church is a pedestal sundial from the former Hall, and to the east in the churchyard extension stands an Elizabethan sundial surviving from the old manor house. In spring the churchyard is bright with masses of snowdrops followed by a carpet of primroses among the headstones. In its elevated position the church has an elegant and felicitous appearance.

COSSALL *St Catherine*

This small church stands at a tight bend in the the little hilltop village. The churchyard is secluded, trim and green, with an entrance through the traditional lychgate, built as a memorial in 1928. Adjacent inside the churchyard is an interesting obelisk commemorating three Cossall men who served in the cavalry at the Battle of Waterloo. (In St Mary's Church, Orston is a drum from the same battle).

The body of the church was subject to a rebuilding in 1842-43. It is recorded that the cost was borne by the Vicar the Rev. Francis Hewgill. Cossall was a parochial chapelry annexed to Wollaton and Rev. Hewgill was Rector of the latter. He also established the school at Wollaton and such munificence is an indication of how well off most country clergy could be in those days.

Cossall is generally remembered for its D H Lawrence connections - the writer born at nearby Eastwood. Next to the church is Church Cottage the former home of the Burrows family. For two years from 1910 Lawrence was engaged to fellow pupil teacher Louie Burrows, daughter of Alfred and Louise Burrows. The village features in Lawrence's novel 'The Rainbow' where it becomes Cossethay - "It was the cottage next . . . the little old church with its small spire on a square tower."

The low west tower is C13 work, plain and of two stages, relieved only with simple belfry windows and a battlemented top. The masonry is local ironstone and noticeably pock-marked through the erosion of soft spots.

Stained glass window to Isaac and Effie Burrows, Cossall.

The short spire is a later addition, probably C14, with four little lucarnes on the sides. The unusual pattern window on the west side is much later and probably dates from the 1842 works. In the tower are bells dating from 1733.

The body of the church has north and south aisles. The fabric of the nave and chancel are C13 but the two bay arcades are later insertions - low pointed chamfered arches on octagonal columns with moulded octagonal caps. The south side is original C14 but the north side arcade is a copy and looks to be part of the 1842 alterations like the outer walls of the aisles. Likewise the windows of the aisles and clerestory are of this later date. It is recorded that the church underwent alterations in 1718, but what these were is unclear.

The small chancel appears all Victorian inside, the east window bright in bold primary colours but largely masked by the later reredos. Pairs of coloured roundels are incorporated in the south side windows, commemorating the Morteyne and Willoughby families. Beneath the chancel is the sealed vault of the Cossall Willoughbys.

The Willoughbys descend from Ralph Bugge a Nottingham merchant of the C13 who bought an estate at Willoughby-on-the-Wolds, the family subsequently adopting the manorial name. The device of leather bags or 'budgets' seen in their arms being a pun on the original name. Fortunate marriages added the manors of Wollaton and Cossall to their estates in the C14. The only monument in the church is the simple alabaster slab bearing the Willoughby arms but with no inscription. This is set under a low arched recess in the sanctuary and is probably mid C14. The Willoughbys have long moved from Cossall, but they have another memorial near the church in the charming group of almshouses built by George Willoughby in 1685.

The carved oak reredos is the work of Alfred Burrows. The family are further commemorated in stained glass windows. The one in the east end of the north aisle is to Alfred d.1948 and his wife Louisa Ann d.1954. Another window in the east end of the south aisle is "a thank offering" from them dated 1947. There are more C20 windows in the aisles. The only ancient glass is the small fragment of C15 work depicting the patron St Catherine, set in a surround of modern plain glass.

In relief above the chancel arch, is a Victorian Royal Arms.

The font is C15, an octagonal bowl with a panelled battlemented design, set on an octagonal base with quatrefoil panels.

NOTTINGHAM St Barnabas

This early Victorian church in Gothic Revival style was built as the new parish church of Nottingham for the Roman Catholic faith. Work began in 1841 and the church was consecrated and opened on the 27 August 1844. It was not until 1850, following the restoration of a Catholic Hierarchy in England, that the diocese of Nottingham was created and St Barnabas's became the Cathedral church with the first Bishop being enthroned in December 1851. The Roman Catholic Faith had been suppressed in England following the Reformation and its adherents could only continue to practise in secret, and at risk, for the next two hundred years. Revival in Nottingham had its origins in a small group that used to meet secretly at Aspley Hall in the 1760's. In the 1770's they met occasionally in the Willoughby family town houses in Nottingham. In 1778 the Catholic Relief Act legalised priests to practice their ministry again. In 1791 a Second Act permitted the erection of chapels and a tiny one was built in King's Place off Stoney Street. Following a steady increase in numbers a new one was built in George Street in 1828 (still standing but converted to other use). With the explosive expansion of the Nottingham population at that time, in only a few years it was clear than an even larger church was needed. Nottingham was intolerably crowded due to the tightness of its boundaries and land was at a premium. Eventually a site was found just outside the then boundary, on Toll House Hill at the foot of the Derby Road.

Augustus Welby Pugin (1812-1852) was commissioned as the architect for the new church and the building cost was estimated at £16,400. Of this the Earl of Shrewsbury, a leading benefactor of new Catholic churches, gave £7,000.

Pugin was a remarkable figure, a man of many talents, great charm and relentless energy, born in 1812 the only son of a French emigré. The father was a talented draughtsman and a keen student of Gothic work. Augustus Pugin from an early age made drawings of buildings and details for his father's publications. By the time he was twenty he was celebrated for his historic costume designs for the theatre and had established his own firm making furniture and carved details in wood and stone for buildings. In 1834 he was converted to the Catholic Church. By the following year he had become possessed of the conviction that building in Gothic style was an essential Christian duty, and had acquired a burning desire to restore the Catholic Church in England to the apparent glory it had before the Reformation. He embarked that year on a career as an architect with very little formal training. The Gothic Revival style in the later C19 and

St. Barnabas, Nottingham, 1841.

since, developed almost wholly from Pugin's zeal and initiatives. Although he achieved some fine architecture in his short life and career, his greater influence is in the roles of author, theorist and decorative designer of furniture, metalwork, stained glass and surface ornament.

The most important building, and most well known which involved Pugin, was the rebuilding of the Houses of Parliament after its disastrous fire in 1834. Pugin helped Charles Barry prepare the competition drawings. Barry won, and from 1844 until he died, Pugin was employed by him to provide designs for interior decoration, fittings and fixtures and to supervise their installation. An enormous task evidenced by the hundreds of surviving drawings. Pugin always worked at a punishing pace and burnt himself out at the early age of 40.

Up to 1840 Pugin had designed principally in the Perpendicular style (c.f. St Mary's, Derby of 1839) but he then turned to the earlier Decorated and Early English styles, feeling these gave simpler motifs. St Barnabas's is designed in Early English style and built completely in ashlar facing. The plan is mediaeval cruciform like a large parish or town church, boldly massed, with three chapels at the east end in parallel and another, the Blessed Sacrament Chapel lying to the west of the sanctuary. The east end of the chancel is dominated by a large wheel window. The other windows in the church are lancets, with very tall ones to the transepts. The coloured glass was designed by Pugin and executed by Wailes. The nave is of 5 bays with pointed chamfered arches on octagonal piers with moulded caps to the arcades separating the side aisles. Roofs are steep pitched. The elements of the church are massed up from the east to the tower and spire standing above the crossing. The dominant tower and spire are also the most ornamental features of the exterior, with paired belfry windows and large corner niches at the base corners containing statues of St Peter, St Paul, St John and St Barnabas. Bands of surface ornament decorate the planes of the spire.

Detail at base of spire, St. Barnabas, Nottingham.

Inside, much of Pugin's original furnishings have been altered to suit liturgical change. The rood-screen was unfortunately removed for the repositioning of the altar to a central position, but the original hanging "testa baldacchino" survives. Most of Pugin's interior decoration has gone, covered over with modern plain paint, except in the almost overpowering colour and gilding of the Blessed Sacrament chapel. This is not entirely original Pugin since it was re-decorated in 1923 and redone again in 1974. But it was carried out by John Hardman Studios, the firm still surviving from Pugin's day, with whom he had close connections.

Pugin was not entirely happy afterwards with his design for the church saying - "it was spoilt by the style restricted to lancet . . . the result is the church is too dark." Nevertheless, despite this self criticism the church is an important example of this remarkable man's creativity.

ARCHITECTURAL PERIODS AND STYLES

GLOSSARY

Period	Dates	
Saxon	7th century – 1066	)
Saxon-Norman	c1060 – c1100	) Romanesque
Norman	1066 – c1190	)
Transitional	c1175 – c1200	
Early English	c1190 – c1300	)
Decorated	c1290 – c1360	)
Perpendicular	c1350 – c1485	) Gothic
Early Tudor	c1485 – c1547	)
Late Tudor	c1547 – c1603	
Stuart	c1603 – c1689	
Jacobean	c1603 – c1625	
William & Mary	c1689 – c1702	
Anne	c1702 – c1714	
Georgian	c1714 – c1837	
Victorian	1837 – 1901	

These are general dates and not precise divisions. Changes of style and trends over-ran in time so there is overlap of characteristics.

The Gothic styles were studied by the architect Thomas Rickman, who in 1817 was the first to classify and give them names, which are still in use.

Rickman also has a memorial in Nottingham in the lofty tower of his St. Stephen's church, Sneinton 1838-39 - respectable Early English character, and a landmark in its smoke blackened state.

Almsbox	a locked wooden box with slot for putting in coin gifts for the benefit of the poor.
Altar rails	were gradually introduced after the Reformation to protect the altar after the removal of rood screens.
Apse	a semi-circular end of a chancel or chapel.
Arcade	range of arches on piers usually dividing the nave from the side aisles.
Ashlar	masonry wrought to even faces with square edges.
Aumbrey	plain rectangular niche in wall originally covered with a wooden door and in which the altar plate was kept.
Baldacchino	free standing canopy over an altar (also known as ciborium).
Ball Flower	ornament of a globe shaped flower of three petals - early 1300s.
Beakhead ornament	an ornamental feature of Norman period, of a row of bird or beast heads with beaks biting into roll mouldings.

Bell cote	turret to carry bells, usually at west end of church.	Easter Sepulchre	an ornamented structure, always on the north side of the sanctuary - the blessed sacrament was placed in an opening within on Good Friday and remained there until Easter Day.
Box pew	typical C18 furnishing of high panelled enclosures to keep out draughts during lengthy sermon services of the period.		
Chancel	east end part of the church.	Entasis	a very slight convex curve to overcome optical illusion of concaveness, usually used on classical columns.
Chantries	small enclosed chapels containing an altar where the Mass could be said for the souls of the founders or, as a guild chapel for the members of the guild.		
		Squire's or Family pews	for the Lord of the Manor or Squire in country churches. With high sides, a door, and often a canopy roof - inside developed into very cosy places with padded seats, carpets and even fireplaces. Examples exist from the Elizabethan period to the Georgian.
Choir	the easternmost arm of a cruciform church.		
Clerestory	upper part of the nave walls above the adjacent aisle roofs, usually pierced with windows to light the nave.		
		Fillet	narrow flat band along a roll moulding or along a shaft.
Colonnette	a small column or shaft in mediaeval building.	Finial	top of pinnacle or bench end, generally carved into leaf form during the Gothic period.
Crocket	decorative ornament of leaf or ball shape placed on sloping sides of angles of spires, pinnacles and gables.		
		Gargoyle	a projecting spout to throw roof water clear of the wall. Usually carved with mediaeval humour into fanciful forms of monsters, figures and grotesque faces.
Crossing	space at insection of nave, chancel and transepts in a cruciform plan, frequently with a tower above.		
		Grisaille	a mainly white glass, thinly painted with black foliage patterns - sometimes with spots of colour. It was introduced in the later C12.
Dog tooth	typical Early English ornament of a series of raised pointed stars set along a hollow moulding.		

Hatchment	a deceased person's coat of arms painted on a lozenge shaped framed panel. Usually C17 or C18. Were hung in front of the house of the deceased and later taken into church to hang on the wall.		accommodate the setting in of a commemorative brass.
		Merlons	The solid parts of a battlement, the openings are crenels.
		Misericords	Ledges under seats in the chancel stalls on which clerics could rest or lean while standing during the interminable services of mediaeval times, usually carved with great skill in inumerable variety of subjects - the whole range of mediaeval life.
Headstones	old ones survive but none are older than late C17. Before then, the churchyard cross represented the buried deceased.		
Herringbone pattern work	mainly stonework arranged in zig-zag courses, but can also be of bricks.		
		Nail head	squared, late Norman ornamentation with raised centre pyramids in a continuous band.
High altar	before the Reformation these were of stone. The tops sometimes still survive, identified by the five consecration crosses cut into the upper face. After the Reformation they were made as wooden tables.		
		Palimpsest	– of a brass memorial, where the plate has been re-used by turning over and newly engraving the reverse.
			– of a painting, where later painting overlaps and partly obliterates earlier work.
Lucarnes	openings or lights in a spire.		
Mass clocks	a simple form of sundial found carved on the walls of early churches. Were used to tell the time for services. Frequently without a fixed finger (or gnomon) and were used by inserting a stick in a hole in the middle.	Parclose screen	side screen enclosing a chantry chapel or the chancel.
		Piscina	a drain, usually in a niche in the wall with arch above and stone carving, used for washing the priest's hands before consecration, and for the rinsing of the chalice. Free standing piscinas on a column are rare.
Matrix stone	stone top of a tomb or monument with a recess cut to		

Poppyhead	fleur-de-lys shaped carved wooden decoration above the end of a bench.	Spire/Steeple	a steeple usually refers jointly to the tower and spire. Spires can be Broach type - where small pieces of inclined stonework cover the triangular space at the corners of the tower. Needle or parapet spires are usually thinner, and rise from the centre of the tower roof allowing a walkway round.
Prie-dieu	a kneeling desk for prayer.		
Reredos	ornamental screen behind the altar.		
Respond	a half pillar attached to a wall and bearing the end of an arcade arch.		
Rood Screen	divides the chancel from the nave and so called because sited beneath the great rood or crucifix.	Squint	apertures usually sited at an angle through a wall so as to give a view of the altar during a service - either from outside the church or where otherwise obscured from inside (also known as Hagioscope).
Royal Arms	usually painted on a square board or canvas, they became general under Elizabeth I. After the Restoration of Charles II they became compulsory in churches.	Tester	a flat canopy over a pulpit, but can also be over a tomb.
		Transepts	wings of a cruciform shaped church.
Sanctuary	the easternmost part of the chancel in which the High Altar stands.	Triforium	middle storey of a church treated as an arcade - either a blind one or with wall passage behind.
Sedilia	seats invariably of stone and usually three in number - set in the wall to south of the altar, used by the priest, deacon and sub-deacon - may be recessed or standing forward - can be canopied and richly carved and ornamented.	Tympanum	the surface area between a lintel and the arch above.
		Waterholding base	early type of Gothic base to a pier.
		Wheel window	a circular window, the earlier form of a rose window.
		Volute	spiral scroll - angle volutes: a pair turned outwards at the corners of a capital.
Soffit	underside of an arch - or may be called an intrados.		

BIBLIOGRAPHY

Nottinghamshire - Buildings of England series	Nikolaus Pevsner	Penguin	1979 ed
Train on Churches	Keith Train	BBC Radio Nottingham	1981
Nottinghamshire	Henry Thorold	Faber & Faber	1984
Nottinghamshire - The King's England (1938) series	Arthur Mee	Kings England Press reprint	1989
Mediaeval Monasteries	M W Bishop	Notts County Council	1989
Norman Nottinghamshire	M W Bishop	Notts County Council	1986
Tudor Trail in Nottinghamshire	G Beaumont	Notts County Council	1992
The Norman Architecture of Nottinghamshire	C E Keyser	British Archaeological Association Journal	1907
A Prospect of Southwell	Norman Summers	Kelham House	1988
The Leaves of Southwell	Nikolaus Pevsner	King Penguin	1945
Slate Headstones in Nottinghamshire	M W Barley	Thoroton Society Transactions Vol. 52	
Nonconformist Chapels and Meeting Houses – Leics., Notts. and Rutland	C Stell	Royal Commission on Historical Monuments	1986
Mediaeval English Alabaster Carvings in Castle Museum, Nottingham	F W Cheetham	City of Nottingham Museums	1973
The Mayflower Story (1957)	Edmund F Jessup	Whartons, Retford	1984
Royal Arms in Nottinghamshire Churches	J. and K. Moir-Shepherd	Rosemary Pardoe, London	1989

FURTHER READING

The Parish Churches of Mediaeval England	Colin Platt	Secker & Warburg	1981
The English Parish Church	Gerald Randall	Spring Books	1982
English Church Architecture	Mark Child	Batsford	1981
The Beauty of English Churches	Lawrence E Jones	Constable	1978
English Parish Churches	Edwin Smith, Hutton, Cook	Thames & Hudson	1976
Local Styles of the English Parish Church	Sir Wm. Addison	Batsford	1982
Perpendicular Style	Dr John Harvey	Batsford	1978
Cathedrals and Abbeys of England & Wales	Richard Morris	Dent	1979
English Church Craftsmanship	F H Crossley	Batsford	1941
Church Furnishing and Decoration	Gerald Randall	Batsford	1980
Discovering Church Furniture	Christopher Hoskins	Shire	1980
Masons & Sculptors – Mediaeval Craftsmen	Nicola Coldstream	British Museum Press	1991
Glass-Painters – Mediaeval Craftsmen	Paul Brinski	British Museum Press	1991
Painters – Mediaeval Craftsmen	Paul Brinski	British Museum Press	1991
Wall Paintings	E Clive Rouse	Shire	1991
Stained Glass	Michael Archer	Pitkin	1979
Church Monuments in Romantic England	Nicholas Reuney	Yale	1977
English Churchyard Memorials	Frederick Burgess	SPCK	1979
Church & Parish	J H Bettey	Batsford	1987
Our Christian Heritage	W Rodwell and Bentley	George Philip	1984
Pugin	Phoebe Stanton	Yale	1977